VOYAGES

AN ANTHOLOGY

Creative Writing Class of 2018

U.F.O.'S

Last Saturday our house was invaded
By smoke and fumes and oil unsaturated!

Our adventurous father was at it again
Only he wasn't searching
For little green men.

He was cooking breakfast
And if you followed your nose
You'd see the stove was covered
With U.F.O's!
(Unidentified Frying Objects)

John Evan Carson

Voyages
Copyright 2018

CBA Publishing Services, LLC
cbapub.com
First Edition

Edited by John E. Carson and Christine M. Brown
Layout and design by Christine M. Brown
Cover design by Anna Talyn

ISBN-13: 978-1-7324746-2-8
ISBN-10: 1-7324746-2-1

TABLE OF CONTENTS

"Shine, Shine, Moon while you can, for you'll soon be conquered by man. You look so beautiful out there in space—but you'll never look the same with man on your face."—Eva B. Carson 1969

INTRODUCTION

With the holidays fast approaching, the 2018 Creative Writing Class takes a look back on an amazing year that has revealed some awesome talent among its attendees; not all of whom are represented in this anthology.

Attendance in the class remained steady as we blasted off into space aboard the USS Gutenberg and explored the solar system on a journey that stretched the imagination of the students and produced wonderful results, some of which you will find in this volume. The tables were filled at almost every session. Several students saw their work published outside of this work, thanks to our allies at *Old Huntsville Magazine* and CBA Publishing Services, LLC, our sponsor and newly launched publishing service company in Huntsville, Alabama.

CBA Publishing Services, LLC, the publisher of our three previous Creative Writing Class anthologies, has lent the services of its Editor-In-Chief, Christine Brown, almost every week of the last year. Christine has been an invaluable assistant and liaison to publishing opportunities to several of the students who sought an outlet for their work.

In addition to helping both the instructor and the students of the class, Christine has also volunteered her services at the gift shop on days when the class was not in session and her busy life allowed.

This year again, she offers her editing and layout skills in the design and production of our class anthology.

The class was also blessed with a second appearance by guest speaker Skip Vaughn, Editor of *The Redstone Rocket* and sports reporter for AL.com. Skip is also the author of the popular book, *Vietnam Revisited,* a collection of interviews with local Vietnam and Vietnam Era veterans. His talks were so liked that no one cared to take a break and even kept him after the class.

Publisher of the *Old Huntsville Magazine,* Cathey Carney received the same rapt attention when she made her second visit to the class. With a circulation of over 25,000 in Huntsville and around the country, The *Old Huntsville Magazine* has been publishing stories about the Tennessee Valley area and Huntsville since 1989 and has found many of them here in this class. Look for it to be on all around Madison county and remember that all monies collected go to benefit local charities and youth groups through the Golden K Kiwanis club.

Old Huntsville Magazine has given us permission to reprint stories from the magazine in this anthology and we thought it appropriate to do so with entries from Belinda Talley, Marijke Given, Tom Carney and others.

In addition, I have been asked repeatedly to share more of my poetic writings and you will find several in this issue.

Thank you for buying and reading this anthology. Your purchase helps fund our efforts to provide what has been and continues to be a popular and important class that strives to help empower people of any age achieve their writing goals.

God Bless and Happy Holidays!

John E. Carson

2018

BREAKFAST ON MARS

What will life be like
When we live among the stars?
When we fly space ships
Instead of driving cars?

When we're above the blue
And the sun seems far away
When the moon no longer rises
To mark the end of day.

As we watch the planet Earth
Turn in harmony
Will we tell the time
Electronically?

The freeways become flyways
Shared with asteroids
It's not just other drivers
That we must now avoid...

Will life be that much different?
Is it only scenery?
Will we still do the things
We do habitually?

Will we spend our Saturday nights
Cruising intergalactic stars
To wake up Sunday morning
And have our breakfast on Mars?

JOHN EVAN CARSON

Don't Push It

"You did exactly what you were not supposed to do, Agnes! Now, there is no telling what you've gotten us into." Wide-eyed and anxious, Reba leaned her face against the rounded square port hole that had been securely riveted into place. "I asked you nicely, would you follow the instructions? Why do you have to be such a rebel?"

With eyes fixed on the calm strobing light ahead and both hands firmly attached to the safety bar, Agnes argued, "Me! I would be having sweet dreams in my own bed right now if it hadn't been for you. For Heaven's sake Reba, it is 7:30 in the morning! I was not the least bit interested in your so-called Early-Bird Senior Saver, much less the new exhibit at the Space Museum. I've don't even like space or astrology, never have and never will!"

Pointing her finger, Reba corrected Agnes. "It is astronomy, the study of space, stars and planets, not astrology. Astrology is about the zodiac signs; I don't believe in that mess. Agnes, I told you, don't push it, don't push that button, but you didn't listen, you never do!"

"Reba, this was your..."

"ALL SYSTEMS GO!" Warnings flashed as the alarm sounded.

Intensity increased, brightness grew bolder, furiously flashing faster, faster...

Loudness rumbled, senses were shaken, baby blues bulged, as the pressure rose...

Ignition flashed, lightening dashed, chest smashed, faces crashed...

Black silence paused, as a gentle glow flickered, low roars began to hummmmm.

Slowly, oh, so-slowly, Reba turned her head barely left. Agnes cautiously leaned her head toward Reba. For a few moments time stopped, they both blinked, paused and stared at each other.

With a muffled voice Agnes whispered to Reba, "You okay?"

Tilting her eyes up, then down, Reba signaled that she had survived.

Their eyes widened in horror when the dull thud of a comet made contact.

Burdensome breathing, oxygen dropping, blackness-blurred, shivering darkness, consciousness defeated...

"How long did we sleep, Reba? You're the teacher, you are supposed to have all the answers. Where are we anyway? This Special Space Day of yours was not such a good idea. I'm cold. You wanted the window seat, where are we?" demanded Agnes. "Brrrrrrr...I should have brought my full-fur coat."

Leaving a smeared spot on the glass, Reba pressed her nose against the window to get a better view. She immediately commenced to crossing her arms and rubbing her hands up and down to sooth the chill-bumps. "I'm about to freeze to death, how am I supposed to know where we are, it's as black as the ace of spades out there! We could be in Alaska or Antarctica for all I know. Dang it, Agnes do something, hold me, do anything, just get me warm!"

A solar flare slightly singed the edge of their transport casting them too close for comfort. A silver intensity reflected from what seemed to be bowls of ice. Reba attempted to peer out the window as the sun crudely unlocked the dark, one crater at a time. The mercury rose rapidly.

"Get off of me, Reba! I am burning up," as sweat dripped down Agnes' back.

"Would you let go? Move your arm! What were you thinking Agnes? Obviously, you weren't! Squirming, Reba tried her best to untangle from Agnes.

Why are you all over me anyway?"

Soaked in perspiration, Agnes began to survey her yellow polyester pants and her pastel plaid shirt. Upon closer examination, she noticed random blotches of what looked like strawberry jam. She thought it was quite odd, because they had not eaten since leaving "The Home" earlier that day.

They met for bagels and coffee at 6 am when the Busy Bean Café opened. Agnes was still disturbed by the look in Reba's eyes and how she tensed up when Ramundo passed them. He spun around on his heels and flashed his charismatic, one-dimple smile in her direction. "Top of the morning to ya, me lovely ladies." Ramundo bowed, as we walked past.

What am I missing? Agnes thought to herself. What was it between the two of them? Agnes could sense an emotional connection in Reba, but not so much in Ramundo.

"Agnes!" Clapping her hands, Reba, raised her voice, like she used to, to control her classroom. "I am talking to you. Agnes-to-earth come in!"

"Don't yell at me, Reba, I'm right beside you." Agnes turned to face her and immediately pulled back in disbelief. Her slowly inching smile rapidly burst into laughter as Agnes couldn't believe what she was seeing.

"Just what is so blasted funny? It's not enough that you nearly killed us, but now you seem to find an abundance of humor in our present predicament."

"Oh, Reba, lighten up, for Heaven's sake," patting Reba on the hand. "First of all, about the buttons, there were three."

"I am completely aware of the three button levels. What possessed you to push level three? I told you, don't push it!"

"Let me explain Agnes, just listen. Level one was for beginners, surely, we are better than that. Level two was intermediate, not us at all and three was for the experienced."

"Agnes we were not experienced, it was our very first time to ride The Mercury Madness."

"Reba, I figured, we're old, we've already experienced it all, besides how bad could it really be? So yes, I did. I pushed the button."

"Well, you darn near killed us both and I find no humor in that, at all!"

"Reba, that's not the funny part. If you could see yourself, well, just look at me, look at my pants and shirt. I didn't spill a strawberry shake, that's from your hair. Ahem, it used to be your hair. Now we're both wearing your Nice n' Easy hair rinse, what color this time, Reba? Raging Cajun Red? I'm sorry, but that's funny stuff. We both look like we've been baptized in The Raging Cajun River."

Eventually remembering where they parked the car, they both slid in.

"Reba, let's put the top back, come on, makes me feel young, besides we won't mess up our hair. It wasn't like we had a 'Magic Carpet Ride,' we barely escaped the from the Pits of Purgatory with your Merciless Mercury Monster."

They waited for the convertible top to snap into place.

"Hey Reba, is your new phone an Apple or an Asteroid? Mine is an Asteroid, not that it matters, we hardly know how to use them. Can I play the tape? Where is it Reba, that country song we like?"

Rumbling down 565 toward "The Home", Agnes and Reba begin singing Alan Jackson's hit song, "Gonna buy me a Mercury and cruise it up and down the road."

"Hey dad, look at that old antique brown car, with those two old ladies."

"Son, that is not just an old brown car. That is a vintage classic, a 1974 Saddle Bronze Mercury Comet."

Belinda Talley

Editor's note: This story was written as part of the Creative Writing Class assignment during their journey through the solar system. This week was about the planet Mercury and students were asked to come up with a creative way to incorporate what they learned into a story. This is also an excerpt of the author's book currently being written. There are several such stories throughout this anthology by the students during their journey to different planets.

HOPE

When life gets rough and we are sliding down,
When friends turn their backs and we wear a frown.
Hope is waiting to carry us through,
Hope is our friend when our life seems blue.

Hope is the confidence things will improve,
If more of us have it, mountains we can move.
Hope is expectation that life can still,
Hold the dreams that life should fulfill.

Spring is the hope of a new beginning,
Life after death that nature is winning.
The seasons are changing the stage we are on,
But we write the script ourselves, one on one.

Hope is the rope that pulls us through life,
Depression and hate only act like a knife.
Cutting the fibers slowly with each passing day,
Making our supports weak, causing us to sway.

Maintaining hope gets us through strife,
Sometimes it is all that holds us to life.
Take good care of it, nurture it well,
Hope is precious, it will never grow stale.

Hold hope close to your heart and never let go,
When you really need it you will certainly know.
Accept it, embrace it, let it come in,
It will take you past sorrow, it will help you win.

Sandy Ballas

On How Things Have Changed:
Memories from Georgia and Ben

Things have sure changed since 1941, and these are some of the ways they have changed. I remember back to the age of six years old. We had no shoes; we could not afford them and had to go without. But going to school without shoes was not looked down on. Now we wear shoes every day, sometimes two or three pair! When we went to school, often times we had no food. Now kids get food every day at school, both breakfast and lunch. Children today often have their own rooms, but if you were a family of five you had to share a room, and clothes too. The clothing we wore back then was often made by our mother, but now we buy clothes in the store. We used to walk miles to get to school every day, through fields and woods and gravel roads. Sometimes we rode mules and horses. Now we walk on paved streets with sidewalks and ride the highways in nice cars. My, things have changed.

We used to work in the cotton fields in the hot sun during the summer time bailing hay, and in the winter time pulling cotton bolls for just about $5 a day. Now we have inside jobs, so we don't have to do that anymore. There was no air conditioning back then and 90% of the houses were shotgun houses; one would open up the front and back doors, so a cool breeze would flow through the building. There were no Burger Kings or McDonalds, families sat down at the table together and ate a dinner that their mothers prepared for them. And there were smoke houses to help preserve meat instead of freezers. Sundays were a time of families going to church and get-togethers. I remember back to the days when schools, restaurants, and other public places were segregated. Blacks used to have to sit in the back of the bus, but now you can sit anywhere you want, and mothers were mothers to all the children in the community.

Thank God things have changed.

Georgia Everson

Remember When?

```
E  V  R  E  S  E  R  P  M  E  M  O  R  I  E
S  A  R  E  L  M  I  F  E  G  L  N  W  Q  U
Y  E  F  Y  H  O  A  I  A  E  K  M  U  I  S
B  M  E  V  G  T  Y  D  D  C  C  O  I  H  N
W  B  M  G  V  H  V  O  E  B  L  Q  C  B  O
Q  Q  Z  C  X  E  S  B  S  E  H  T  O  L  C
I  U  G  H  E  R  Y  H  A  L  F  G  T  L  W
S  C  H  O  O  L  N  Q  O  X  J  P  R  E  R
F  A  M  I  L  Y  S  H  T  E  X  X  Z  E  N
W  B  H  F  Z  K  M  B  O  C  S  N  H  M  L
F  L  P  O  R  V  P  N  I  R  O  O  O  H  F
I  D  G  H  C  R  U  H  C  T  S  L  S  A  R
D  C  Q  S  V  S  Y  O  T  B  T  E  W  V  E
A  L  A  B  A  M  A  O  Z  S  C  L  S  M  R
W  G  T  A  U  X  C  U  E  X  H  U  D  J  Y
```

ALABAMA   HORSES
CHURCH   MOTHER
CLOTHES   PRESERVE
COTTON   SCHOOL
FAMILY   SHOES

POTUS vs The Prime Minister

To the British, loyalty is so archaic

For they believe it to be very prosaic

Not part of their mosaic

But we hold to this notion

With tenacity and devotion

So thank Goodness for the Atlantic Ocean

Tom Mailey

The Party Line

Seated on a bench in the mall the other day, it occurred to me that teenaged girls have two things that are more important to them than air; i.e.; clothes and a phone. Every young girl I saw had a cell phone in her hand and almost everyone had a bag from one of the trendy stores that carry young girl clothing items. It has been this way for a long time as I remembered my teen years.

Country kids ride to school on a big, yellow school bus with the name of their school and a number painted on the side of it. The bus arrives the same time, or about the same time, every morning and is waiting for you in the parking lot when the last bell rings. Failure to find your correct bus can lead to a very long ride to nowhere near your house. The seats are narrow and close together and only two people are allowed to sit in one seat. This was a challenge for me because the clothing style at that time included can-can petticoats. These were made from net, starched so stiff they could have stood alone and worn under circle skirts that served to make getting into those bus seats almost impossible even if no one else was sitting there. My best friend lived a few miles down the road and was always on the bus by the time I got there. This day she wasn't.

Being a Senior in high school was a very important position to hold in the school and on the bus. Younger students would move and let you sit where you wanted most of the time. Thank goodness because this particular morning my can-cans were especially stiff and my circle skirt was quilted. Once at school the day went by in a normal fashion. We had PE at 1 pm and had to change into one-piece jump suit uniforms which left all our clothing in the girls' locker room. Of course, the can-

cans would not fit in the lockers so they were piled on top. After some outside track events, we arrived in the locker room to find our can-cans gone! This was not funny. No one can wear a circle skirt without lots of petticoats or it is about six inches too long but we did not have a choice. Once in the hallway from PE, we found the can-cans. They had been tossed so they stuck on the fluorescent lights up and down the lower floor hall.

This was a big mystery and funny to everyone except the owners of the can-cans. I needed to call my friend right away to tell her all about it. However, the only phones were in the office and to be used for emergencies only. There was one more hour until school was out and a thirty-minute bus ride before I could call Sheila and tell her all about today. I could not wait to get to bus number 86 and home to a phone! Sitting was much easier as I did not have my petticoats.

The bus pulled to stop and I ran across the street to my uncle's house and the only phone available to me.

The phone sat on a table in the living room by the couch. I ran through the kitchen door, tore around the kitchen table and headed down the hall to the living room. Grandma called a greeting and did I want a snack. I was not sure I really heard her in my haste to make that call. The phone was a heavy, black instrument with no exterior way to call a number. The receiver was heavy enough to be used as a weapon if you needed to knock someone out cold. In order to make a call, there would be an operator who asked, "Number please." After grabbing the receiver off the hook and expecting to hear an operator ask me for Sheila's number, I heard, "…and that dish she made for Sunday was awful." Mrs. Peacock was on our party line.

Quietly the receiver was replaced back on the hook but my frustration would not be quiet. I walked back to the kitchen, hugged Grandma and made a couple of loops around the table while telling her about what had happened at school. She giggled and understood why I had to use the phone. By this time, I was sure the conversation was over so back down the hall I went. This time when I tried to call I heard, "….and that is not all." Really? That had to be all. I was not as careful this time when I hung up the phone but let it click loudly so Mrs. Peacock would understand that there was another call waiting. I decided five minutes should be long enough to wait so I pet the dog, fed the chickens and rushed back inside for my third attempt at telling Sheila all about the funny sight. There seemed to be silence when I picked up the phone this time but Mrs. Peacock said in a loud voice, "This must really be important" and hung up. Hurray!

The operator asked for a number please and after hearing it ring twice, Sheila was finally on the line. I was so excited in telling her about all the goings on that day until I heard her say, "I know. Donna just told me." Disappointment flooded every fiber of my being. I absolutely hated that party line.

Betty Pettigrew

A True Untold Story

New Mexico has had many mysterious and unusual stories about things the locals see and hear. Here are some that are talked about to this day:

The best known is the Roswell UFO Crash on July 2, 1947. The government initially notified the press that a "flying disc" had crashed there. After it was published in the local paper, the government corrected the story to debris from a weather balloon. Many years later to something even harder to believe.

March 1948, a flying saucer may have crashed in Hart Canyon northeast of Aztec. Witnesses reported finding a large, superbly crafted disc, and discovered 14 to 16 (depending on who you ask) charred, small humanoid corpses from the wreckage. The government sent a team of scientists to recover the bodies and investigate them. Of course, the scientists were sworn to secrecy, so their findings still remain unknown today.

A few Taos residents claim to hear a relentless humming noise like a "diesel engine idling in the distance." Called the Taos Hum, the sound has puzzled investigators from Los Alamos National Laboratory and Phillips Laboratory at Albuquerque's Kirtland Air Force Base. Both have been unable to identify it.

Other amazing stories mention an underground lab, jointly run by alien species and the U.S. Government outside Dulce in northwestern New Mexico.

Then there have been about 24 sightings of Big Foot. Some by Jemez Springs residents, around the Valles Caldera National Preserve.

How about Prehistoric birds known as Teratorns flying around Las Cruces? Witnesses have reported seeing the monstrous birds as far back as the 1800's and have seen these raptors with twenty-foot wingspans as recently as a couple years ago.

About ten years ago, my husband Norm and I were driving home to Tularosa, New Mexico after spending the day in White Oak, New Mexico. White Oak is considered a ghost town, but has a little church, started by a western artist. It was an hour from where we lived in Tularosa and we went to the Cowboy Church the last two years we lived in New Mexico. It was so much fun to stay and visit with the other members that we would stay until dark most Sundays. We had no idea that we would have a memorable experience in the middle of nowhere going home.

White Oak is about 12 miles from Carrizozo and it was another 45 miles to Tularosa where we lived. The Trinity Site where the first nuclear bomb was tested on 16 July 1945 was not too far from Carrizozo. Trinity is part of the White Sands Missile Range. The Missile Range includes 3200 square miles in five counties in Southern New Mexico. Next to it is The Valley of Fire where there are lava flows from 1,500 to 5,000 years ago.

As was our habit when leaving White Oak, we stopped at a station in Carrizozo to get a soda or juice to drink on the way home. We had no idea when we got in the car that we would have one of the most amazing and disturbing experiences of our lives.

It was dark and we didn't even check the time since we were only going home. We loved the ride home on Route 54 that ran past the Three Rivers Petroglyphs Site about 28 miles south of Carrizozo and 17 miles north of Tularosa. We seldom saw any other vehicles on the way home and once in a while we would see a train in the night to our left and higher off the road. But not far from Carrizozo, the road flattened out for the rest of the trip home. Usually we could see scrub brush close to the road and shadows of some deserted building here and there.

Those green road markers were on the side of the road, but we never cared about looking to see how much farther we had to go. We were talking about the day we had and what we talked about with the people we were with that day. Such a relaxing day until we saw what I will try to explain to you.

Norm was driving our fairly new Mini Cooper S and we weren't that far from where we bought our beverages, but far enough for it to be absolutely dark. It must have been a cloudy night because usually you can see a lot at night in the desert by the brightness of the Milky Way. We later figured we were between 5 to 10 miles south of Carrizozo, but that was only a guess. When something shocks you to your core, you have trouble with stupid details that you wished you would have paid attention to right away when you had the chance.

We might have been talking before it happened, but when we saw it we were quiet. I remember I spoke first, "Did you see that?" in an excited, but quiet tone. It seemed like Norm didn't hear me and then when I was about to ask him again he said, "Yes." It is hard to remember our words exactly after that but we said if we were not together at the time that we might not believe it happened. We were so grateful that we experienced it together because it would be hard to explain to each other.

Validation of something unusual . . . well absolutely something impossible. Out of this world so to speak. We started comparing notes. We were cautious about doing even that. We didn't want to make it into something exaggerated or crazy. We strove to stick to just the facts that we were sure of and not add what may or may not be true. But, we also wanted to compare what each of us saw so we could remember to write it down (which we didn't do right away).

When you have an unusual experience you almost never do what you should or meant to do. However, we came up with the following set of facts that we agreed on.

* We only saw it in our headlights.

* It was 8 ft tall (we didn't want to exaggerate).

* We only saw it from the right to the left of the two-lane road with no shoulders to the road.

* It crossed in two steps – one on each leg.

* We did not see the feet, shoes, or whatever it had.

* We couldn't describe the legs, but the knees were bent backwards like a chicken. (The 1997 movie "Contact" with Jodie Foster had a character of a young boy that jumped up on the roof of a building after reversing the bend of his knees to that of a chicken so he got more leverage.)

* We didn't see any face or beak or nose or anything where any of those would be.

* It was wearing a cloak with a hood that seemed to be gray in color that reached to just above the bend in the leg where a knee would be.

* It was very fast and didn't turn to look left or right.

* The time to cross the road was like click, click—so fast.

We weren't afraid but we were excited more and more as we talked about it. We tried to keep it to just the facts so it wouldn't change what was real. We sent the info to Linda Moulton Howes at Earthfiles.com to see if she had ever heard of anything like we saw. But no response.

Someday, we would like to be hypnotized and recorded to see what each of us would say after freeze framing the event in our minds. It may give us more clarification of what we were actually seeing.

In the meantime, I would like to find someone in the Huntsville area that knows where the 7 to 8-foot statue of Big Foot is that I saw the first week of December 2016. I saw it when we were driving around with our realtor looking at homes to buy. It was on a property in a business park area, but I didn't say anything about it at the time because my husband and she were talking. They didn't see it and I would really like to know where it is and why it is there with a fence around it.

Sandy Ballas

He Said What?

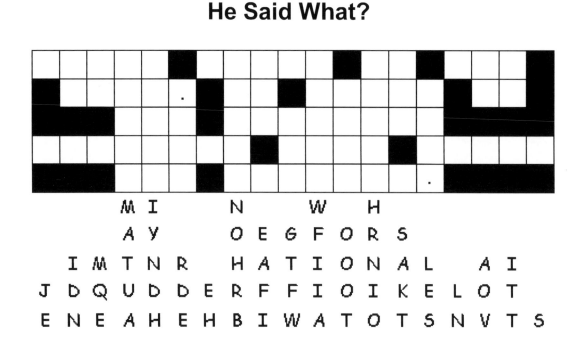

— M.J. McGuire in his book *101 Fake Books You Must Read Before You Die*

(Fallen Phrase: Move the letters up in each column and unscramble to reveal the fallen phrase.)

Road Trip

Dawn was about to break
As we started our trip out of Huntsville
Toward Highway 72 E for the three hundred odd miles toward
Somewhere called Kingsport in nearby Tennessee.
Our rental car appearing to be
The lone traveler on the darkened roadway.
With only moonlight, like a light house beacon,
To show us the way until the headlights
Landed upon embedded reflectors in the pavement.

"Not a creature was stirring,
Not even a mouse"
Except for the three of us girls
Three generations
Together, at last,
For our first ever all girl road trip.

It seemed as though the whole world was asleep
Like my granddaughter on the back seat.
The store lights were off and
Only their signs made us aware of their presence –
Together with the string lights which hung over car lots
Swinging in the already sweltering Alabama breeze.

Occasionally we were met by another traveler
Who meandered through a blinking traffic light
To join us for a few miles
So we could follow each other's tail lights
And play catch up and pass
To avoid the boredom and tedium of a pre-dawn trek
Without caffeine and not enough sleep.

Yawning is the tune played for many a mile
When nearly alone on an open road
And there is no CD player,
And the radio stations keep going in and out of reception
Through the hills and dales of this stretch of highway –
Unless you like "hillbilly".

Cognizance resurfaces
When passing an open gas station or convenience store or
When coming across an interesting billboard or
The highway sign which read, "Get Hammered, Get Nailed,"
Newly displayed for the long holiday weekend.

Then you glance at the speedometer –
Look for a trooper –
Proceed with caution –
Grateful for the escape, this time –
Until zombie-like,
You get back in that zone and
Catch yourself –
Swearing it won't happen again.
When suddenly,
Your side seat navigator,
Who has been nearly comatose the whole time,
Is awakened by the motion which comes
After coming out of steep curve
Tells you,
"It's your ticket."

Patricia Woolfork

Road Trip Part 2

Deep within the grasp of darkness
One must find ways to combat the feeling of
Impending insanity
Caused by the monotony of the insipid drone of the
Soundtrack playing ping pong inside your skull...
"How much longer?"
"Is that all the farther I have gotten?"
Et cetera, et cetera, et cetera.
You watch the clock on the dashboard
And try to remember what time zone you are in.

I choose to focus on the change of colors in the sky
As morning light dances with the waning moonlight
And fog descends from the mountaintops
To form the dew that plants kisses on the ground below –
The first signs of a new day approaching.

Streaks of orange appear in the horizon
As the sun slowly begins to manifest itself
And stirs my resolve to have a better day, today,
Than yesterday.

The sky is turning from black to navy to azure
As the sun grins through the reappearing clouds
Which have been shrouded in the darkness.
Birds, in flight, have arisen from their slumber
To find sustenance for their young
Before the summer's heat overtakes us all.

In that moment, I remember. . .
I have been blessed to live to greet another day.
I have been given another chance
To become a better version of myself.

I remember . . .
I am covered by Grace,
Bestowed with Mercy,
Protected by Sacrifice,
To be a true reflection of His Goodness.

His presence is in the fully risen sun
Shining brightly above a mountain in the distance,
Casting its reflection on scattered tributaries,
And now streaming though the car's visors
As if to say,
"Good Morning."

Car after car join me in parade down the highway
Toward jobs in factories and offices,
Car lots, and convenience stores –
Giving me more reason
To be mindful of our safety and the destination
On this road trip called life.

Patricia Woolfork

Ninety-Eight and Counting

With the American Legion approaching its one hundredth birthday in March of 2019, the historic Clayton E. Moneymaker, American Legion Post 237 closed its doors at the end of May 2018—just a few days past Memorial Day, and after completing work on the new Honor Guard Van meant to serve the families and veterans of Huntsville and Madison County.

Dating back to June 1920, Post 237 was established under a temporary charter as the Peter Crump Post and immediately began serving the veterans of WW1 in Huntsville and Madison County and has continued to do so throughout the decades since.

The first American Legion Post in the state of Alabama, Post 237 was granted a permanent charter in 1926.

Closed its doors? After 98 years of service? How can that be?

After many changes in its name, location and number designation, Post 237 finally found a permanent home with the construction of the present building at 2900 Drake Avenue S.W. in 1983.

That building has served as the meeting place for the many other veteran organizations in Huntsville who do not have a Post Home of their own.

What would become of them and the Honor Guard that has served the city and County for so many years? Indeed, Mayor Tommy Battle recently issued a Proclamation dedicated to the thirty-year Honor Guard Commander, Jerry Lankford, who was forced to retire for health reasons.

Why the new van if the doors were to close? Who would honor the departed veterans if the only fully uniformed Veteran Honor Guard no longer existed? The van, acquired from the DAV (Disabled American Veterans) of Huntsville, was recently given a makeover by local business, Signs by Tomorrow at 1035 A Putnam Drive, who also provided Post 237 with a new entrance sign to the parking lot; both at very low cost to the Post. Retaining some of the original graphics, SBT transformed the van's DAV identity to the American Legion, Post 237 designation and added the Honor Guard lettering. The new Honor Guard Commander, Jerry Rains, completed the painting and restoration on the van, finishing the work just in time for Memorial Day.

And then, just two days later, the doors closed! And when that happened, 80-100 volunteers from Home Depot began work on a restoration of the property. The building's exterior received a new, bright coat of paint, landscaping and footlights for the corner sign and restoration of the flag poles. Inside, the ballroom was completely renovated with new paint, light fixtures, carpet and dance floor. Work was also slated for the social quarters by members of the Post. At an estimated cost of $32,000.00, the bill was paid by Home Depot as part of its Spring Project.

After ninety-eight years, a grateful community has come together to thank Post 237 for its many years of service by giving it the best birthday present possible; A new look and a new life—and those closed doors were re-opened just two days later and will remain so for many years to come.

John E. Carson

The Gristmill

The gristmill is laden with water for power, belts and wheels turning the stone for the owner.

So many sounds of comfort I find as I dig my toes in the moss aligned. I listen and hear the crank at the crown of the wheel as it turns round and round dumpin' water back in where it was found.

It groans as it strains and I wonder the stress of 200 years more or less.

Oh, what it's seen I'd like to know; the shadows of men so long ago, maybe rebels were killed on these banks or slaves may have hid under the planks. You are old enough to see Indians moved and maybe you hid some of these under you.

Were you ever a sawmill or wood shop or gin? I can't imagine how much there has been.

How did you sell all that flour and grits? Did they ride to the rail to sell what you did? Were there important people to carry corn too like Col. J. Acklin, Steele or Calhoun to name just a few?

I know you saw the end of the war in 1861, they had to restore.

Keep turning old gristmill we'll always love you for your grits and your cornmeal will feed families too.

Carol Wells Barnette

Opposites Attract

Did you marry a baby? Evidence backs up the personality differences between the oldest child versus the baby of the family. The first-born child is typically a protective, take charge, domineering, and cautious achiever. Most of the time the last born, or baby, of the family will tend to be fun-loving, care free, and want to be the focus of attention.

Close to a year apart, he was born in 1912 and she in 1913. The oldest of eleven, Buna Ovella Maddux desired to be strong and set a good example for her younger siblings. Thomas Edward German didn't have the pressure that is put on the oldest child. He was more of the happy-go-lucky type and the youngest of four.

Three miles south of town, past several crop fields and down a dirt road, was the old home place of Tom. He didn't know Buna, even though their farm was just up the road. Her family lived in a better area because their farm was closer to town.

A dinner-on-the-ground church picnic was the first time he saw her. Tom was nineteen when he spotted her sitting on a pretty handmade quilt. He knew then and there he would do whatever it took to win her approval. Later he would find out that all those kids sitting with Buna were her brothers and sisters. Tom was immediately smitten by her beauty and grace. Buna, on the other hand, was busy chasing after all of her younger siblings and didn't give him much thought.

Communication in the late 1920's was tricky, but Tom was determined. He sent word that he would come calling on Thursday about sundown. Buna wanted everything perfect…but with ten younger children in their five-room house she knew it would be quite a challenge.

Back toward the corner in the floor of the front room was a huge heap of black-eyed peas that were drying for seasonal storage. The process required the bean pods be beaten and stirred daily. When the hull was dry, the peas inside would begin to rattle. Eventually the peas would separate from the hull and fall out. Those peas were not part of what Buna had envisioned for her date with Tom, but she had no way of telling him not to come.

The smaller children had completed their daily chores and Buna didn't waste any time recruiting them to help. You should have heard the rattling as those black-eyed peas went to flying! It was a sight to see…all of the sifting, shelling, and shaking to sort out that mountain-peak pile of peas.

The sun began to set, and Tom showed up as promised. There they sat, in the front room…where many little eyes were secretly watching. (Not a black-eyed in the bunch.) Tom and Buna dated on and off for several years. The big day eventually came, and he asked her to marry him. She said yes, and plans were underway.

Buna's mother and father were quite relieved. They wondered if any of the kids would ever leave! You see, she was the oldest and the very first one to leave home, and she was twenty-seven!

Buna, like every bride, wanted to have a beautiful wedding. But with very little money, it would be difficult. She looked and searched, to no avail. Tom was aggravated and blurted out, "Well, why don't we just get married on Guntersville Bridge?"

Tom had never before experienced the look on her face. Buna had a twinkle-in-her-eye as ideas began to saturate her mind. Then came the "ah-ha" moment. Buna had always loved being outdoors and around all of God's beautiful creation.

The birds were singing, the Tennessee River was slowly flowing, and the sun was beginning to rise over the mountain. June 23rd, 1940, my parents were married…at sunrise on Guntersville Bridge.

The story isn't over. Fast forward 30 years.

Another first-born child and another baby of the family fell in love. A family tradition was repeated. The birds were singing, and the Tennessee River was flowing as the sun rose on that Sunday morning of September 6th, 1970. William Tom Talley and Belinda Joyce German were married at sunrise…on Guntersville Bridge. TV cameras captured the historic event as the 300 guests were serenaded. Yes, music was played from a boat on the Tennessee River beneath the bridge. History was repeated. Like mother, like daughter.

The George Houston Bridge in Guntersville served the area well for its 64-year lifespan. That bridge would provide passage, connecting and joining people and families together. Only two wedding ceremonies were performed on that bridge…and both saw the sunrise.

Wait…you thought the story was over? No, we aren't quite done. Fast forward another 33 years.

The baby of our family meets another first-born child. They fall in love and the decision is made to be married. Problem; the bridge had been torn down. Besides, this bride, and sunrise wedding would not work well together.

On May 31st, 2003, with 200 witnesses and a few random strangers with their dogs, Pastor Rusty Nelson performed the wedding ceremony of Adriane Ovella Talley and Jason Stanley Kulvinskas at Big Spring Park. In the east side, the historic part of the park, there is an iron bridge. Yes, the ceremony was on a bridge. The time of day? Sunset, of course! Like mother, like daughter…like mother, like daughter. History does repeat itself.

My parents were married 49 years when my mother went to be with the Lord.

Tom and I have been married 47 years. My daughter, Adriane and her husband, Jason, have been married 15 years. Seems to me that bridge weddings really do connect people pretty well. Well, at least it is true in our family.

We all know that opposites attract. A first born marries a baby of the family. But we also know that marriage is not always wine and roses…

My husband winks at me and says…

"Our wedding on the bridge…I should have jumped off!"

…Opposites attract, but sometimes opposites attack!

What does the future hold for this family tradition? Perhaps ask one of the five grandchildren if they like bridges.

***

In the summer of 1954, Tom and Buna German opened a fabric store in Huntsville called The Cloth Basket, a successful fabric business for 35 years.

Tom and Belinda Talley live in Huntsville. Belinda has worked with local seniors for 17 years and retired in 2017 to pursue her dream of writing. When asked what she would like to write about, she gave a mischievous smile. "Oh, I have numerous tales about our escapades and adventures. Don't you think for a minute that seniors are done living. No siree! When we're together…we're all eighteen again! I have more stories than I have time. Wait for it, there's more to come."

Belinda Talley

Those Were the Good Old Days

Those were the good old days.

We stayed outside until the street lights came on.

We rode our bikes, jumped rope, played kickball and hopscotch.

We got scrapes and cuts.

We got hosed with iodine and mercurochrome.

We were obedient to our parents.

We didn't talk back even if we knew or thought they were wrong.

We had chores to do.

We had to earn our allowance.

We had to do our best in school, or suffer the consequences.

We'd rather die than get detention after school.

We said prayers in school regardless of religious denomination.

We showed respect to our teachers and administrators.

We went to school to learn.

We were disciplined, but we learned to accept the rules.

We asked permission to speak when grown-ups were talking.

We had to say yes/no ma'am and yes/no sir to our elders.

We did everything as a family.

We ate our meals together.

We ate what was put in front of us or nothing at all.

We said grace.

We said our prayers before bed.

We turned the TV off.

We had real conversations with each other.

We read and studied scriptures and worshipped together.

We did not know what "dysfunctional" meant.

We had music that meant something.

We still hear it being heard today.

We had good, clean fun.

We made life-long friends.

We had pride even if we had little.

We respected ourselves and others.

We took advantage of opportunities offered to us.

We became contributing members to society.

Those were the good old days.

Patricia Woolfork

OUR MISSION

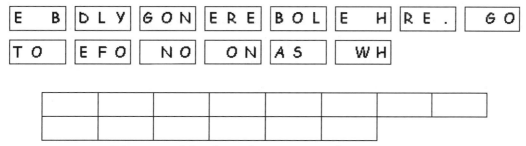

Unscramble the tiles to reveal a message.

Hey! Mr. Bullfrog You Are Back

Hi, Mr. Bullfrog, it's good to see you and hear your bullhorn voice again. I was afraid those sharp bladed machetes had got you while those determined Green Giant Landscapers were tiding up the dead reeds from around your home. After that I didn't see you anymore!

Thank you, Mrs. Rogers for your concern. I hid that first day in the muddier part of the pond. My biggest concern was keeping the Green Giant Landscapers from spotting our launching ship.

Mr. Bullfrog! What! Our! What! Launching ship! What!

Well, Mrs. Rogers many things are done in miniature nowadays and us Green Team Bullfrogs have aspirations too. Green Team has been working for months on a launch platform that would take the USS Gutenberg, our space ship, to those bright objects in the sky. The juiciest bugs we may ever eat may live on those bright objects. The only obstacle was that they were a little higher in the sky than your ordinary pond delicacies. So anyway, that night after the whirlwind of machetes used by the Green Giant Landscapers stopped for the day, Bullfrog Green Team completed final plans for launching. We all decided early the next morning before machetes started whirling again some Bullfrog Green Team members would stay behind and guide me to rendezvous to Mercury. After launch success my Green Team temporarily moved to a new location till the agreed upon time for me to return home.

I was speeding thru space at lightning bug speed. Expectations were high and soon USS Gutenberg would land. Landing on Mercury was like landing on a fish hook. Sharp, uneven, rocky surface was dark gray and covered by a layer of dust. Water was not found anywhere or mud or tasty delicacies to feast upon. The small, bright shining light seen from Earth was large and blinding on Mercury and the heat, oh my, hotter, than an Alabama summer.

Since Mercury would rotate back to the landing spot in 88 days, I decided to stay at that location sitting in USS Gutenberg and observing other bright objects as they passed by. If there were any delicacies out there my observation window would get splattered with a new and exciting anomaly. In the meantime, while waiting for other bright objects to pass by, I discovered Mercury was either extremely hot or extremely cold, no in between. The sun rose twice and there was always two sunsets and that occurrence would keep the most studious bullfrog confused. As the days went by and we passed other bright objects, none produced one little savory bug. On the 88th day, I radioed my Green Team on Earth that I would be returning home on schedule.

Boy, Mrs. Rogers it was so good to be back to the family pond that had some new reeds growing and the bugs were flourishing again. Mrs. Rogers, you know something else, remember that old adage, the other side of the fence isn't always the best, there's something to it. See you another day, bye for now.

Bye, Mr. Bullfrog, glad you had a safe trip.

***

The warm summer sun filled the air as I strolled along the small inviting pond where Mr. Bullfrog lived. As I was about to pass the pond, out of the corner of my eye was a hopping movement. I had not heard or seen Mr. Bullfrog for some time. Mr. Bullfrog saw me coming and came out of his camouflaged part of the pond to say hello.

Mrs. Rogers, it's a delightful day for a stroll.

Hello, Mr. Bullfrog, the new growth of reeds around the pond really helped mask your green-brown body. It also looks like the growth has increased the abundance of food.

Yes, indeed Mrs. Rogers, I am very glad. My family has multiplied since we last spoke. I now have a 100 grandchildren and one of my sons who completed astronaut training became a Green Team member. While still on Mercury, that son, Whiplash, and other Green Team bullfrogs also who had completed astronaut training, all arrived on a shuttle to rendezvous with the USS Gutenberg. Using a remote manipulator arm to transfer the new crew members and supplies was like a South Korean Bullfrog using his sticky tongue to catch a small snake; slow, cautious, and precise work.

Wow, Mr. Bullfrog that's impressive news! What was it like living on the USS Gutenberg?

Mrs. Rogers it was like living in a six-bedroom house that has two bathrooms, a gym, and a 360-degree bay window. When you first get inside the spacecraft you may end up with a bruised ego. You are so excited to be aboard and your movement skills are not yet as controlled. It is easy to bump up against a piece of equipment on the wall held by Velcro and it accidently falls loose or you bump into other astronauts. Eventually you become adjusted to traveling back and forth to do your work inside the spacecraft.

We wake up each morning at the same hour by music. We cleanup, have breakfast and start our assigned duty for the day. The bath routine is for those who need one. Bathing is done by using a special soap that doesn't clean off with water. Shaving; Bullfrog Green Team doesn't do that either. Bullfrog skin stays as smooth as a hairless worm. Brushing our tiny hacksaw blade teeth is a most pleasurable duty. I fill my mouth with water sucked thru a straw, slush the water around before adding paste, shut my eyes and imagine being submerged in water from my pond back home. After a moment of bliss, I spit the water and paste into a washcloth. Breakfast consists of freeze-dried water beetles and snails and doctored up with a dash of Tabasco sauce. In space, food no longer tastes like it does on Earth so we spice it up a little with Tabasco sauce. After breakfast, we begin our assigned tasks. Some astronauts are assigned to take out the trash. There are three dry trash bins on the USS Gutenberg and will be transported back to Earth and one for wet that is recycled on board. Some astronauts are assigned to vacuum, some wipe everything clean, still others maintain equipment inside the spacecraft and outside. Keeping the USS Gutenberg clean and maintained is an extremely important component of space life.

Some of our Bullfrog Green Team was assigned to continue searching for food sources and some had the assignment to discover ways to help astronauts get the prescribed eight hours of sleep per night. Consistently, astronauts report an average of six hours of sleep per night. Bullfrogs don't sleep. Did you know that Mrs. Rogers? We were perfect for the assignment. Several different approaches were studied. Science shows the use of sounds can impact our well-being. A case in point is the "Sonic Attack", on the US Embassy in Havana when employees reported dizziness, cognitive difficulties, headaches, and hearing loss, among other medical issues. Bullfrog Green Team purposed the use of high and low frequencies that sounds balanced and natural, stuff that provides a sense of normalcy. Also, we wanted to see if controlling body temperature helped. Most astronauts sleep in sleeping bags that are strapped to the wall to keep them from floating around at night. We suggested sound proofing the sleeping bag to keep out spacecraft noise and using controlled sound and temperature. We have a theory that deep inside the subconscious mind when the mind is not engaged, there is a semblance of fear where possibly the use of sound would facilitate an eight-hour sleep. Controlling the temperature inside the sleeping bag was also recorded to see if body temperature would facilitate a longer night sleep. Another purposed theory was to record findings from sleeping upside down. Something as simple as sleeping upside down may enable astronauts to get the desired eight hours sleep. Another important part of astronaut duties is exercising two hours every day to maintain body muscle and body mass. I can only imagine if Bullfrog Green Team didn't exercise our already skinny arms and legs would mummify and our dry skeletal body would be used in a training session for what not to do. Lunch and dinner was more freeze-dried food spiced up with Tabasco sauce. After dinner was over and before bed time we all had free time. Some played Chess and Scrabble. Games such as Chess and Scrabble allowed for the ability to detach from seriousness and monotony of being "trapped" in a potentially dangerous workplace. Some astronauts called home, still others played DVD's.

Thanks, Mr. Bullfrog that gives me a great view of life aboard a spaceship. What was the flight pattern for USS Gutenberg?

We were headed toward the planet of love, Venus, Mrs. Rogers.

The next time we meet would you tell me more about your spaceflight?

I would be happy to Mrs. Rogers, bye for now.

Bye, Mrs. Bullfrog.

***

It was a rainy day in Alabama and the rain was coming down in buckets as I watched from my post-stamp patio. I watched big frogs and small frogs out enjoying the down pour of rain. Rain infuses a climate of romance among frogs and provides them with an easy target of snacks. After heavy rains, a plentiful supply of slimy, dark, wiggly, worms come out from their tunnels underground to the surface and can easily be munched away by hungry frogs.

Up over the manicured, grassy, knoll in front of my post-stamp patio hopped Mr. Bullfrog. Hey, Mr. Bullfrog, I called out. Do you have time to tell about passing Venus today?

Hi, Mrs. Rogers, I have been enjoying this romance induced day along with tasty snacks. I'll stay for a short time.

Hop up here and plant yourself on my secluded porch lined with green, dense, bushes, Mr. Bullfrog.

From Earth that bright shiny star twinkles from above and actually seeing the much-acclaimed planet of love and beauty from the space ship USS Gutenberg stirred our hearts and minds. We all gathered for a short time on the observation deck and our bullhorns started blowing. How do you keep bullhorns from sounding off? We trained for this if it happened.

Our mission was to collect more data from the mysterious surface of Venus, sometimes regarded as Earths sister planet. There were similarities to Earth hidden below the dull yellowish cloud of carbon dioxide and light amounts of sulfuric acid shrouding Venus.

Mr. Bullfrog, does it rain on Venus?

Yes, Mrs. Rogers it does, but not the type of rain that it does on Earth. It rains sulfuric acid, the stuff that would change our green, brown, and yellowish coats to chitterlings you couldn't find let alone eat.

Have you ever got caught up in a love triangle? On Earth, I am as contented and passionate toward my spouse as anyone could be, but in space and close to Venus the mystery under her clouds tugged at my heart strings. As we stood on the observation deck of the USS Gutenberg, orbiting by Venus, I felt the presence of

Suadela, the goddess of persuasion in the realm of romance, steering me thru the clouds into another dimension. Breaking thru the clouds veiling Venus, I landed on Maxwell Montes, Venus' highest mountain. Viewed from there were other volcanic mountains, vast ridged plateaus, and a couple of highlands. The reddish-brown surface overpowered me with her presence. Burning with passion I proceeded deeper toward the core of Venus. I observed a rainbow-like features known as "glory". Glories typically comprise a series of colored concentric rings on a bright core.

When turning away to explore other areas, I heard love and beauty calling me to stay, come back, don't leave me, there is still more areas to explore. As I traveled forward, warnings of danger ahead was heard from afar. As I disappeared from sight, a lightning flash startled me and I fell into a nearby dry crater. Temptation again surrounded me, but a different kind of beauty. Persephene was quickly by my side comforting me. She is known in the underground world as enchanting and beautiful. As time passed I became enamored with my surroundings. I struggled with needing to return to the USS Gutenberg with new data, and realized the beautiful, beguiling Venus would soon destroy me when she saw Persephene also wanted me. Just then I felt as if someone was shaking me. It was Whiplash, my son, handing me my duty assignment. Exploration of Venus discovered some tantalizing discoveries and Venus being a multi-faceted planet will keep us coming back to learn more of her secrets.

Mrs. Rogers, the sun is beginning to appear thru the rain clouds and it is time for me to go home.

Thanks for sharing the discoveries with me, Mr. Bullfrog.

***

The sun was disappearing from Earth's range and soon the stars would be shining bright. Children were being called home for supper and to get ready for bed.

Two young boys began reeling up their fishing lines from within the pond. For a brief time, they had been fishing in the neighborhood pond for anything that would bite, the same pond Mr. Bullfrog called his home. I went down to the ponds edge to see what the two boys had caught. They said just some tugs on the baited hooks under the surface of the murky water that made the red and white bobbers slightly bounce. They picked up the fish bait and headed home.

The vegetation casting shadows around the pond was almost gone. Darkness filled the night and stars lit up the night sky. Standing by the pond's drainage tunnel, I gazed at the brilliance above. As I looked down, out from the tunnel hopped Mr. Bullfrog, along with other family members.

Mr. Bullfrog, what were you doing in that barren, concrete tunnel, I asked.

Lighting strikes us dead, but fish hooks mutilate us, said Mr. Bullfrog. We all hate it when someone fishes in this pond. My eyesight is poor now and makes it hard to distinguish a fine bug specimen from a piranha, aka, fish hook. Everyone living here is on high alert until they leave.

Mr. Bullfrog, I know Mars is often called the red planet, named of a Roman god because the reddish color reminded people of blood, it is terrestrial, also follows an egg shape path, rather than a circular orbit like other planets. I would sure like to learn more about Mars.

Mrs. Rogers, discoveries about the red planet started in ancient times. Since Mars is visible from Earth with the naked eye it is almost impossible to tell who first discovered Mars. Egyptians, Babylonians, Plato, Dutch, astronomers all contributed observations about Mars. Galileo was the first to use a telescope, designed by him, to observe the goddess of War, Ares, so named by the Greeks.

Mr. Bullfrog that is amazing to learn exploration of Mars started in Ancient times.

Yes, since Ancient times the advancement of modern technology continues and scientist has seen some extraordinary results. Exploration of Mars atmosphere and surface will continue for many years. The accumulation of research sustains the belief that life may have existed and encourages the belief that life can be established on Mars.

Stories of aliens existing on Mars have prevailed for years and knowing about the settlement on Cydonia Plains, Bullfrog Green Team was ready for anything. As the USS Gutenberg orbited closer to Cydonia Plains, the landscape looked like Roman ruins. The arena type walls had crumbled to the ground as well as the building surrounding the arena. Nearby was a statue of a large frog ready to jump. Someone or something had dropped their helmet in a hurry to escape whatever demolished the buildings or was it left by someone or something who had taken the helmet off to show respect as they knelt at the foot of three erected crosses? The scene only invoked more questions than answers.

We can only imagine a battle having taken place between two opposing forces. One force returning to living in emerging harsh planetary conditions, possibly leading to extinction, and the other force seeking ways to survive.

Roberto Orosei, the co-investigator on Marsis (Mars Advanced Radar for Subsurface and Ionoshere Sounding) said water was discovered on Mars. Marsis was able to detect echoes from beneath the Southern polar cap of Mars that were stronger than surface echoes and interpreted this data as indicating water below. He also suspects water exists in other locations on the planet.

Bullfrog Green Team's theory is that to preserve their species, eggs was preserved in bubble wrap type protection from harsh elements and sunk to the bottom of the South polar ice cap where they would stay in a frozen condition. Those forces remaining and seeking ways to survive messaged to a friendly spaceship near Venus that soon would be returning to Earth. While on Earth they would learn how to deal with deteriorating conditions at home and gradually return to their red planet with terraforms to build a lunar base for research and retrieving from under the Polar ice cap their deposit of eggs.

Mrs. Rogers, do you believe there are aliens living and working among us? You decide.

There has been a few convincing testimonies from people swearing they have seen aliens, Mr. Bullfrog. Some of the UFO sightings could be aliens transporting terraform to begin building lunar bases. That is a crazy thought, on that note I better get inside before some alien comes. Good night, Mr. Bullfrog.

Good night, Mrs. Rogers.

Sally Rogers

The Longest 76 Hours

Grant Baze, my cousin, looked every inch a United States Marine: Tall at 6 foot 2; dark with black hair and a permanent tan and an easy white smile. His name, Grant, was not a matter of whimsy for that side of the family were direct descendants from General William Tecumseh Sherman. Because of his great admiration for General Ulysses S. Grant, he insisted that the first male of each generation be named Grant.

Grant was a 17-year-old high school senior in Arlington, Texas, when on December 7, 1941, the Japanese attacked Pearl Harbor. Too young to enlist, Grant lied about his age and was admitted into the U.S. Marines. After basic training he was assigned to the Second Division and was sent to the Pacific.

At an age when most boys are getting a driver's license or learning how to invite a girl to a dance, or even how to behave in the back seat of a Ford, Grant was learning names like Iwo Jima, Guadal Canal, or the worst of all, Tarawa.

Lying 2,400 miles south by southwest of Pearl Harbor are the Gilbert Islands. The Tarawa Atoll, or just Tarawa, is part of the Gilbert Islands and here two great forces would collide: The Empire of Japan and the wounded United States. The Japanese High command decided that it was here that the American advance across the Pacific would be stopped. This island is two miles long and 800 yards wide.

The Pentagon, on the other hand, decided that the Japanese forces must be removed to provide safe passage for B-29's to bomb Japan. They named this Operation Galvanic.

The Japanese selected the finest engineer in the Japanese navy, Rear Admiral

Tomonari Saichirn, to construct the fortifications. He intended to stop the Americans in the water and if not there certainly on the beaches.

To achieve this, he constructed a series of deep trenches around the Island to facilitate the movement of troops without detection or casualties. Also, the 1,500 Korean slave laborers at his disposal, worked intensively for a year to construct air raid shelters, firing pits and a large number of strategically located pill boxes around the island to provide the defenders with a wide range of fire at the attackers. They constructed an airfield connected by trenches in the middle of the island.

In addition, the Japanese put in place 40 long range artillery pieces to duel with American sea forces and to hit troop ships before they could disgorge the marines. Further, the Japanese had 14 coastal defense guns including four large Vickers 8-inch guns purchased from the British.

When defensive fortifications were completed, Admiral Saichirn was replaced with one of Japan's finest battlefield commanders, Rear Admiral Keiji Shibizaki, who toured the fortifications and announced that it would take one million men, one hundred years to conquer Tarawa. In addition to the 1,500 Korean slave laborers, 6,400 first line Japanese troops packed the defenses.

Among the attacking Americans was the Second Marine Division commanded by Col. David Shoups under the command of General Julius Smith. The American armada included 17 air craft carriers, 12 battle ships, 8 heavy cruisers, 4 light cruisers, 66 destroyers and 36 transport ships.

The attackers would be Red Beach 1, 2, 3, Green Beach and Black Beach as reserve. The attack began at 6:20 am on Nov. 23, 1943. Things began going wrong almost immediately. The invasion force attacked the beach in Higgins boats and LSTs. The attack plan had the landing craft making it to the beach. The landing craft required four feet depth, so the plan relied on an incoming tide. General Smith ignored the advice of an Australian advisor who said that sometimes tides, for some unexplained reason, simply do not always come in.

Consequently, the landing craft hit bottom hundreds of yards from shore. Many Higgins boats could not cross the reef. The light tanks and Alligators were stuck on the sea wall. Others were stuck on the reef. As a result, many marines left their landing craft nearly 500 yards from shore in waist deep water to wade ashore amid withering Japanese riffle, machine gun and mortar fire. On the first day the marines had 1,500 casualties.

A young marine only a few yards from Grant's right took a hit from Japanese mortar shell and simply disappeared. Others were described as looking like rose bushes. Yet the survivors of Green 2 made it ashore, dug in and took defensive positions. Still those marines were pinned down on the beach taking relentless Japanese machine gun and mortar fire from heights around the beach and in the strategically placed pill boxes. To many it seemed like carnage.

Col. Shoups ordered an assault. With too few survivors, the attack was beaten back as was the second assault. Dark fell with marines still stranded on the beach. Rest was impossible. Even with some initial reinforcements, day 2 fared no better. Flanking movements failed for the Japanese used trenches effectively to move troops unseen. Pincer movements were no more successful.

Bombardment was called for on days 2 and 3 but the unseen enemy had moved to other locations. This was the first time in Marine Corps history that the signal went out 'Issue in doubt.' Then all remaining reserves from Black Beach 3 were poured into the battle and gradually the marines, in hand to hand combat, moved off the beach. A more stable foothold had been secured at the cost of many lives. This became known as the longest 76 hours in Marine Corps history. Finally, however, through dogged determination the Marines prevailed and the Japanese died to the last man. By the end of the battle the marines had 3,166 casualties.

Many later questioned the need for the battle and the manner in which it was conducted. One dissenter, General Holland Smith, when asked if the Tarawa was worth it said, "Emphatically, no." He compared this battle to Pickets charge at Gettysburg "From the very beginning the decision of Joint Chiefs to seize Tarawa was a mistake and from their initial mistake gave the terrible drama of errors, errors of omission rather than errors of commission resulting in needles casualties." He added, "A miscalculation of tides and height of coral reefs."

Robert Stroud said, "Tarawa stands alone alongside of the Alamo."

Grant Baze received many medals for valor and bravery. And when he finally retired from the Marine Corps as a Lieutenant Colonel promotable, he had earned those stripes the hard way; not in air-conditioned training sessions, but in bloody combat. General William Tecumseh Sherman was smiling.

Thomas Mailey

Tongue Twister Tales

The Black Bear

I walked along the sandy shore watching sand castles disappear. The tide was in and I could see a dark red sky reflecting on me.

Suddenly twigs crackled and I ran. I ran as fast as I can.

I turned around and behind me a bear, black and bristling in the night air.

Lazy leopard lay ahead, but Frisky Fox was still in bed. The sky was darkening no more red. It was getting quite black instead.

Rabbit Rare regarded me, but he raced away no more to see.

I ran and ran until I saw Sheriff Sharp Shooter to the draw. I heard the blast and turned to see the big black bear bleeding bad blood, but no more was he.

Alice alligator arrived to assist removing him aside was bliss.

Decrepit Daisy dog detest the bad black bear's bleeding death.

Ginny Gander grew aggrieved gruffly grumbled don't deceive.

Frisky Fox foiled the folk foraged forest he forsook.

Lazy Lucy

Lazy Lucy left a lot of unclean things and letters lost.

No comb upon her dirty head. She lay in bed as though she was dead.

Laughter left her long ago. No more friends to find their foe.

My Grandma

My Grandma's love I can't compare. She taught us things and how to share.

Her cellar was a prize to see. The many shelves she canned for me. Peaches and pears and pineapple-cot jam. She canned even more for family and friends.

I'd slip out of bed down the road I'd go before day light. I loved her so.

She'd get out of bed to fix our tea and bake a cake just for me. She was always proper an English Queen sipping her tea with lemon and cream.

Her pain was great she was not well. Her range of ranch stories I remember to tell. She and her brother were best of friends they loved each other until the end. She could out shoot him but that was ok.

He didn't let that get in the way. The stories she'd tell I'll never forget. How life on the ranch was just for the fit.

The night she left she rocked in the chair and laid back her head to rest there. A smile I saw after she closed her eyes at peace with God I did surmise.

Carol Wells Barnette

Marijke's Story

I was raised and went to school in Holland but I was born in 1942 in a Japanese concentration camp on the island of Java in Indonesia.

Indonesia is a group of islands located in Southeast Asia, near Thailand, Vietnam and Cambodia. Indonesia was a Dutch colony renamed the Netherlands Indies in the 17th century when the Dutch started the Dutch East Indies Company. Their ships brought back spices, which were very valuable to Holland and many other European companies. The Dutch kept Indonesia until 1942 when the Japanese invaded the island during World War II.

In 1929 my father went to Indonesia as a forester for the Dutch government. He and many native Indonesians operated saw mills to transport tropical woods to Holland. Other Dutch people operated rubber plantations, coffee plantations, etc. In 1933 my dad went back to Holland on a furlough for a year and met my mother. He went back to Indonesia by himself but asked my mother to marry him. They were married by proxy because my dad could not go back to Holland for the wedding. My father's youngest brother acted as the groom, but only for the ceremony. This type of wedding was very common in those days because distances were so far and transportation was only possible by ship, mostly freighters, so in most cases such a trip took several months. Also, the Suez Canal in Egypt did not exist yet, so the journey had to go around the Cape of Good Hope in South Africa.

They had a good life together until 1940 when they got the news about Germany invading and starting war with Holland and many other European countries. Contact with their parents and family was lost and for many years they did not know whether they were dead or alive. About six months after the war started in Europe, Pearl Harbor was bombed and the Japanese invaded Indonesia.

It was said that Java had powerful troops: Dutch, South Africans and many other volunteers from other European countries. My dad had taken precautions to place the mill under direct military protection and plans had been made that, if necessary, the mill would be dynamited and blown up rather than have the plant operated by the Japanese.

Dad had also decided that it would be safer for my mother, who was pregnant with me, to find a safe place to hide. She left for a small village in the mountains where some of the mill workers lived. She took a small suitcase with some clothes and baby clothes, a handbag with some important papers, their dog, and faithful cook and house servant named Meneh, who had been with my parents for years and was always treated like family.

They still had a car and a chauffeur and so they drove about twenty miles to the isolated village in the jungle. Upon arrival they were greeted by the head of the village who had a perfect place for Mom to hide. It was a dilapidated, run down house where, more than likely, the Japanese would not expect someone to be living. To make it even better, some natives came after Mom, the house servant, and their belongings moved in, and boarded up the windows and doors.

One day, Meneh came back to the house and told Mom that the Japanese were nearby and had set up camp. That same evening Mom heard people outside the house. Lying on her stomach and holding the dog's mouth shut so she would not bark, she could see the head of the village, a Japanese officer, and two soldiers talking in Malayan about the house. Mom, who spoke Malayan, understood the conversation. The head of the village told them that the house had been empty for a long time and that it soon would be torn down. It seemed to satisfy them and they left. This was proof to my mother that the villagers were on her side and willing to help her.

The next day my mother heard a loud explosion and she knew what that meant: The end of their beautiful saw mill, the mill my father had worked so hard in and in one year's time brought back to a well-working and profitable company of which he was so proud.

The following hours were very difficult. My mom did not know what had happened to Dad. Had he fled to the woods? Or maybe he made it to the forestry headquarters in the nearby town of Madioen? Or had he been captured by the Japanese?

Eventually, after a day or so, he showed up in the village and was shown where Mom was hiding and stayed with her until they heard that the Japanese troops had left and that the Dutch army, as well as other volunteers, had surrendered to the Japanese. A Japanese commander and soldiers arrived in a nearby town and all Dutch as well as other white nationalities had to report to military quarters in Madioen immediately. Mom and Dad could now leave the village, retrieve their car from the jungle, and say their goodbyes to the faithful villagers.

When they arrived in Madioen, they were given a place to stay along with thousands of other people until all men and boys over twelve were rounded up and transported to unknow destinations. Some women followed the trucks and found out that they were brought to the train station and loaded up in waiting trains. Some days later, someone told Mom that the men had been interned in a large prison in the city of Soerabaia.

My mother moved into an old house together with six other women and children and stayed there for about two months. Suddenly, two Japanese officers appeared and told them to vacate the house within two days and leave all their belongings behind, so that they could move there themselves. It was up to the women to find a new place to live. They soon found an old house, cleaned it up as best as they could, and made the best of the situation.

Mom had received permission for one of the women to leave the house after the 10:00 o'clock curfew to fetch a doctor or nurse for Mom to deliver the baby if it was during the night. A doctor from Java was assigned by the Japanese to deliver me. All Dutch doctors were imprisoned along with my dad. I was born on June 28th, 1942. Mom was happy and sad at the same time, realizing that my dad was not there and not knowing where he was or whether he was still alive.

In February of 1943, all women and children were loaded on truck and taken to the railroad station. There everybody had to board blinded trains, so nobody could see where we were going. We were taken a long distance to a former Raman Catholic orphanage for boys, hoarded in, and led to large rooms and halls where along the walls spaces and platforms had been constructed and where everyone was given a space just large enough to lay on. The hall Mom and I were assigned housed 224 women and children. Good news came and that was that my dad had been moved from prison and transported to a concentration camp a long distance from where we were. Thank God, at least Mom knew that he was still alive.

In June of 1944, my second birthday was coming up and Mom and I were kept captive in a concentration camp near the city of Semarang on the island of Java. This time we had no clue where my Dad was or if he was alive. Presents were unheard of for birthdays, simply because there was nothing to buy, no stores, no money. Mom met a lady who made small bears out of yellow dust cloths which she had managed to pack into her suitcase that she and other women were allowed to carry to the camp when they were interned. She thought up the idea to exchange the bears with whomever was interested for a bowl of rice or a spoonful of sugar or perhaps a handful of vegetables. Mom managed to get one of the little bears for me and when she gave it to me on my birthday, the bear and I were inseparable from then on. It was my very first toy, the best gift ever, and it changed my life. I named my little friend *Beerie*.

Toward the end of that year, a new order came from the commander; all women who still had any kind of jewelry—rings, gold, silver, or even wedding rings—were to be surrendered to them. Mom had kept two rings hidden so far, one was her wedding ring which she had crocheted wool around and used as one of several curtain rings on a small curtain she had fabricated out of a piece of dress material she had saved and hung up for a little bit of privacy between her and the other woman sleeping next to her. The second treasure was a gold ring with a blue sapphire which was a wedding gift from my dad. She came up with the idea of opening up my little bear, hiding the sapphire ring inside, and sewing it back up. She figured it would be safe there, nobody knew anything about it, and *Beerie* would always be with me.

One day, early in 1945, Mom and I came back from the central kitchen, where we went every day to get our small portions of food—mostly rice and soup. Mom looked at me and noticed that I was no longer holding *Beerie*. When she asked what happened to him and where he was I answered that while we were at the kitchen I had given him to a very sad little girl who was crying because she did not have a toy and wanted to have mine. She was there with her mother I said. Mom was devastated. All she could think of was her ring, not so much about the little bear, my only toy.

She knew that she had to find the lady and her little girl and she was determined to find her—not an easy task to search and question some 8,000 women and children.

By some miracle she found the lady, and the little girl with *Beerie*. Mom pleaded and begged and convinced the lady that the bear had been my birthday gift and the only toy I ever owned. Of course, the ring was never mentioned; nobody knew, not even I. Finally, the lady understood and in spite of her little girl's unhappiness and tears she handed the bear back to me. Both Mom and I were so happy that it all worked out for us.

After we were liberated, Mom managed to bring *Beerie* and the rings back to Holland where she wore the rings often.

When I was about to have my 18th birthday, Mom and Dad had the sapphire ring cleaned and reset and, on my birthday, I was presented with the ring. It was the most beautiful present I had ever received and once again changed my life. Today I still own the ring and wear it on special occasions.

***

When I arrived in America in 1963 with my husband, I was just 20 years old and coming to America seemed like a big adventure!

I had met my husband, Ron, in Spain in a small town called Rosas on the Costa Brava, not far from the Spanish border. Ron was a radar specialist in the US Air Force and stationed on a radar site Rosas. My parents, sister, brother, and I vacationed in Spain on summer vacation several years and that is how Ron and I met. We spent a lot of time together on the beach and talking and decided to correspond and tell each other about our different lives in Holland and in the United States. We did write many letters; there was no email in those days. Ron came to Holland once to see where I lived and grew up. After I graduated from high school, I decided to go to Paris to study French and French history at the Sorbonne. When Ron had leave had he came to Paris to spend time with me. It was then that he asked me to marry him and live in Spain until it was time to go the USA.

We had discovered that our love for each other was the real thing and at the end of September 1962 we married in my home town of Reeuwijk, not far from Gouda. It was a lovely wedding. We rode from my parents' house to the town hall in a carriage drawn by two horses. Family and friends followed behind us in their own cars.

After our wedding, we spent a few days in Holland and then packed up his Volkswagen Beetle with mostly my belongings and wedding presents on the back seat as well as in the trunk. My wedding bouquet and dress were placed on top of the luggage in the back seat so that when we had to cross borders from Holland into Belgium, Belgium into France, and then from France into Spain and we were asked if we had anything to declare, we could just tell the border patrol that we were on our honeymoon and the wouldn't search our belongings. It worked. The border patrol man would look in the back seat and say, "I see your wedding gown, so you must be on your honeymoon." We would smile and say, "Yes sir, we are." "Continue on," he would say.

When we arrived in Spain a few days later, we moved into a small bungalow which Ron had rented for us, until it was time to go to the United States. Our months spent in Rosas were so romantic; if felt like one long honeymoon. Of course, Ron had to go to work on the base, sometimes might shifts. I had to amuse myself while he worked. I took long walks on the beach and in to the town and tried to make conversation with the locals. I did not speak Spanish and they actually spoke a dialect called Catalan. I found that when I spoke French they could understand me well. One day I heard about the only beauty shop in town and decided to make an appointment. They said, "Sure I could come," but I would have to bring my own shampoo, conditioner, and even towels; they did not provide that. I did as they asked and one fine day headed for the shop. As I sat in the chair, I noticed that several local Spanish ladies dressed in black came in and took a seat where they could see me well. Some ladies had brought their knitting in with them. After my shampoo, one of the ladies walked up to me and said, "I hope you don't mind if we sit here and watch you. Your hair is so blonde and beautiful and curly. And your eyes are so blue. You must have noticed here in Spain that we have dark hair and dark eyes." I was very honored and said that I had not objections. It is amazing to me how it seemed that this little village was still so simple and almost behind the times compared to where I came from.

Ron and I loved living in Rosas those six months. Then in March 1963, the day came that we had to leave. Ron was very happy; he longed to go home to his family and friends. He had been in Spain for nearly four years. I had very mixed emotions. I was moving far away from Holland and my family to a country I had never been to and Ron's family who I had never met before. After all, I was only twenty and not very mature. We said our goodbyes and drove to Barcelona and boarded a flight to New York. I could not believe that I was actually going to New York and America. Was it a dream come true? We were able to stay in New York for a few days with a cousin of my mother who lived in the Bronx. He was a wonderful man who had attended our wedding in Holland. He showed us all the sights and also introduced me to hot dogs and hamburgers. The size of the buildings and skyscrapers were unbelievable to me. One can imagine the contrast with Holland where everything is spread out and New York—unbelievable!

Ron was discharged from the Air Force and we left for Cleveland, Ohio, where Ron was from. There I would meet his family and friends in Berea where he grew up and be introduced to the American way of life. After living in Ohio for four years, we moved to Buffalo, New York. Ron was working for Goodyear as a sales manager. This was a promotion for him. Our first daughter, Monique, was born in Buffalo in 1968.

There was another promotion for Ron in 1971 and a move to Dayton, Ohio followed. In March of that year our second daughter, Wendy, was born. Our life was happy and eventful. Over the years we met many people and made good friends and fortunately, were able to keep in touch with our families. My parents, sister, and brother came to visit us on several occasions and Ron, the girls, and I were able to go to Holland. All our moves and changes were exciting and we were able to adjust quickly wherever we went.

Ron was not always home; he had to travel a lot for his job, so often, situations and problems had to be handled by me. More moves followed to Memphis, TN, Morrisville, PA, and Willingboro, NJ. It was here we bought our first home. We love it and were so proud of our accomplishments. We had many friends, belonged to clubs and did so many fun things with the girls. My parents came to stay a while and life was good. We were even members of a large Dutch Club in Philadelphia. They had many activities to keep up with Dutch traditional holidays. I was hoping we could stay there forever and I could now truly say that I loved it in my new homeland.

But it all seemed to good to be true. Ron came home one day and announced that we had to move again; this time to Wadsworth, Ohio, not far from Akron. My world caved in and I felt miserable. I did not want to move, start over, and lose our house that I loved so much, and most of all, say goodbye to many good friends and neighbors again. And how would this affect the girls, who were settled in school and had their little friends? It was exciting for Ron: A new job, new people to meet, new business opportunities and challenges. But, it had to be. All our belongings were packed up into a huge moving van and the "gypsies" were on their way again.

We found a very nice house. Someone Ron worked with had a wife who was a realtor and she was very helpful in finding the right house and neighborhood for us. Once we were settled in and the girls were back in school and Ron on the road again, I sat down one day and cried. I was very lonely; no friends, no family, nothing to do to keep me busy. I complained and argued with Ron a lot and told him that I was going to sit in the house forever. I was not going outside and I was not going to make new friends ever again. I even had thoughts like "why did I ever have to marry an American" and "why did I go so far away from my home and family in Holland".

Then one day it seemed like a miracle happened. The school that the girls went to was having a festival and a parent-teacher meeting. Ron was on a business trip, so in order not to disappoint the girls, I decided to go by myself. When I was there I was not really interested in much nor did I have the desire to talk to anyone. Suddenly, a lady tapped me on the shoulder and said, "Are you Mrs. Given and are you Wendy Given's mom?" "Yes, I am," I said. She smiled and took my hand and said, "Wendy toured the neighborhood and the street you live on, on her little bicycle and knocked on doors and said, 'Would you please be my mommy's friend and meet her? She is lonely and sad. If you want, I can show you where we live.'" Tears came to my eyes and I could not believe that my little girl had observed and noticed how unhappy I was. It opened my eyes and from then on I decided to make friends and be part of the community. And, so I did and the rest of our stay in Wadsworth was fun and eventful. We did not stay, however; after a while we moved back to Buffalo, then North Ridgewill, OH, Athens, GA and Huntsville, Alabama. It looks like we will stay here now. We are both retired and have lived here for almost 30 years.

Marijke Given

*Editor's note: Ron passed away in 2017 and Marijke continues to live in Huntsville with her daughter Wendy's pet bird, an African Gray parrot named Schatze.

Making Pictures Out of Words

I once believed that poems were for people very much different from me. But the world stopped spinning for me for ten minutes back in 1974. I was taking Freshman English 101 when I was hit with a life changing event.

Our English teacher at Jefferson State Jr. College had a very interesting name, Mrs. Box. She was not only very smart, but cute as well. She wanted to introduce her class to the world of poetry. However, my classmates and I were less than excited about visiting this new world of poems. But Mrs. Box, we could tell, loved poetry and wanted to shake up her students' worlds by bring something new into our lives.

Mrs. Box had a number of poems written by fellow classmates of hers while she attended the University of Alabama. During this one class out of many, she picked that one day to ask us to interpret those nameless friends' poems. The instructor handed the person in front of me a handful of poems. I reached forward and took the poems being passed back to me, all the while fearful of making a fool out of myself. Now, let me not be misunderstood. I can read, but unknown to me at the time, I have dyslexia. That word had little meaning to me then, as I had not heard of it in 1974. It wasn't until 1980, after getting married to my wife Rita Kaye, that this had come to my attention.

I had taken a job with the John Hancock Insurance company and paid three hundred dollars for a top of the line answering machine in order to screen telephone calls for this new job. Wow, what a shock! As I would listen to the playback, I learned just what dyslexia was all about. I explained to my wife that I was reversing words and phone numbers while taking the messages. Rita, who was a retired college professor, explained to me just what dyslexia was and aided me in fighting this learning disorder that I never knew I had my entire life. She taught me to screen all of my calls to make sure I had new information correct and to write down everything. That way I could always recheck my numbers, words, and even left and right turns. This helped me greatly, however, reading out loud to others was still painfully slow, no matter how often I would try to read to others or even myself.

That brings me back to 1974 and the poem which I had picked out to interpret. The poems themselves meant nothing to me and I was so ashamed to admit that I would not be able to read due to my stage fright. My only intention at this point was to not embarrass myself. As I glanced through the pages of poems, I was looking for two things. I wanted a short poem, with simple words so I would not make a mistake, and something in the poem that might make it easier to interpret. The shortest poem I could find had 16 lines, and the only thing that meant anything to me was a stanza describing a lone airplane sitting at the end of a long runway.

I read the poem one word at a time, painfully slow. While I was deep in study, suddenly every word came alive to me. In pictures, or flashes, the words very much became images that I could not have known anything about. I poured out what I saw. The poem told the heartfelt story of a young man and his desire to be with his girl and their new baby, but also the need he felt to serve America in the Armed Forces. The thing that shocked me while I was painting this vivid picture with words, was my teacher with her mouth wide open. Only Mrs. Box knew anything about the poem and the young man who wrote it. I was so taken back my Mrs. Box's expression that after ten minutes or so I stopped reading and interpreting the poem for fear I was making a fool out of myself.

That ten minutes of fear I felt landed me a B+ in Freshman English 101 and was the highest grade I ever made in all of my years of school. It also inspired a desire to write in myself. Who would have ever known that a simple poem could make such an impact?

Harold Lee Vest

Escape Pluto

CHIEF SUNNY SKIES

After Dad (1906-1952) died, adults would just pat me on the head and move on, partly because I was so little and shy. Dad was found in a dessert canyon, southwest of Carlsbad, NM, after missing for three months. Two weeks later one of his best friends, an old Indian and medicine man, Chief Sunny Skies visited. Dad always had a knack for becoming friends with unusually interesting people. Chief Sunny Skies (1900-1972) was the son of Chief Big Snake (1861-1948) of the 2,000-year-old Acoma tribe, southwest of Albuquerque. The Acoma Pueblo is reportedly the oldest continuously inhabited community in North America, and possibly the Western Hemisphere. Chief Sunny Skies had to leave the Pueblo because he married a white woman. In 1937, she requested that he move to Carlsbad, NM. He opened the Hitching Post on Canal Street and was widely known as an exceptional artist for his silver and turquoise jewelry.

Chief Sunny Skies explained to me my responsibilities, as the only male in the family. I was now a Brave. It was my duty and responsibility, as a Brave, to make sure my mother and sisters were cared for and protected. He presented me with a Brave's drum he made especially for me. It was 12 to 15 inches in diameter and about five to six inches deep. The chief hand-made it from deer skin he personally tanned and painted with natural dyes. The paintings were of several important symbols that he explained. He was the only person to talk to me as an adult. I have to give Chief Sunny Skies a lot of credit for my behavior and attitude during the process of becoming a man. A remarkable gift.

Ernest "Skipper" Colin

Pilot in Command

Standing there I can feel the adrenalin rush. It's a marvelous sight. In moments I'll be in command of this complex machine. Holding my fresh full qualification license in hand, I am about to embark on my first time as solo commander.

"Time for some calming deep breathing. Slow in, now slow out and push out all the air. That's right," I tell myself. It does help. "Now reach out, interlock the fingers, and turn your palms to the outside and stretch your hands and fingers," I further echo to my mind. "Loosen up."

"Oh Man, look at those twin Gates motors on either side, all that power just *rarin'* to get going. The cluster of meters, dials and knobs just waiting for me. The microphone is mine as I ease down in the cushioned seat with leather arm rests on either side. This feels like sitting on a throne and all I am missing is a golden crown and bejeweled cane and I'd be a King. I am in control. I carefully place the headphones over my ears, and although I could hear OK from the speaker, the headphones take out any other sounds and let the audio come through crystal clear.

"Now remember to speak from deep in the pipes to make your voice sound more resonant and more mature than your years might reveal," I remind myself. I speak into the RCA 77-B1 microphone, talking to 'the single person' to whom I am directing my information and comments.

I have a gleeful sparkle in my eyes and am filled with enthusiasm. Upon the signal, I am off, the motor coming to life in an instant. The Gates engine awakens and is roaring to life. Combined with viscous dampening on the arm, it's smooth as silk on a baby's skin. The arm is equipped with a GE-VR II, the latest in the industry, easily capable of 20,000 if required to do it, but it rarely will be needed. At the same time, it's tough and rugged.

Before I can blink twice, I hit 45 and raise the control up. "Up, Up, and Away."

"The 'Dee Scott' (my air name) is On The Air!"

On my higher right, sit a pair of massive motor PT-6 tape recorders. The take-up motor can break a finger if you get inside the spindle rewinding a tape.

I carefully watch the VU meter hit the 100 mark, but not into the Red Line area of Plus One or higher. If so, terrible things will happen I have been warned. Eight gleaming "pots" on the Gates Yard along with the Master Gain. It's called "The Yard" because this control board is a yard long from one side to the other. My shoulders are rocking from side to side and I feel like jumping out of my seat and rocking my whole body with the music, "Maybe Baby" by Buddy Holly who only recently died in February in an airplane crash.

It was a rush, not much different or less memorable than the first kiss of my life. Those things and the smallest details are embedded in memory, and due to repeated visits, it never gets faded.

As advised, talking to that "one" person you have pictured in your mind and not an "audience" is how to make radio more personal. You are, after all, usually speaking to just one person at the other end of the airwaves. Speak to them in a warm and friendly way. Say things with a giant smile on your face that will make them also smile. I am in command of everything on this flight. and seeing the surging 5,000-watt transmitter behind the glass wall, filling the airwaves with wonderful music, is ecstatic.

It would be exactly twenty years before Charlie Dore would come out with the song, "Pilot of the Airwaves," but I certainly can identify with that song.

On that summer night in 1959 at midnight, alone in the control room of WAAY Radio with my fresh FCC First Class Engineer's License required for directional antenna array radio stations, I was the PILOT IN COMMAND of the Airwaves that night.

M.D. Smith

SPACE TRIVIA

1. What is the name of the force which keeps the planets in orbit around the sun?

2. Which planet is covered by clouds of sulphuric acid?

3. Which planet is named after the Roman god of war?

4. Which planet is closest to the sun?

5. Which two planets take less time than Earth to orbit the sun?

6. Which planet has a day which lasts eight months?

7. What is the term for a natural satellite?

8. Who was the first man in space?

9. Which was the first space probe to leave the solar system?

10. How many US space shuttles are there?

11. What is the approximate temperature at the surface of the Sun?

12. What force bends light rays travelling though the universe?

13. What is almost halfway through its 10-billion-year life, will expand to become a red giant and then shrink to become a white dwarf?

14. Which planet orbits the Sun four times in the time it takes the Earth to go around once?

(answers page 153)

DIFFERENT LIVES, DIFFERENT FACES

I think that one time or another

each one of us sit and wonder

Why this time why this place?

We look in the mirror at an unfamiliar face.

What is the purpose what is the reason?

that brings us to this particular season?

If in this life we change only one variant,

would we know, would it be apparent?

The steady ebb and flow of life might take other directions.

We can only follow along without conscious corrections,

as we drift through lives making connections.

Sometimes we're gone but back again

with occasional visions of who we've been.

We blissfully fathom where each life will lead

as we search for improvements in our life we need.

While in pursuit of a fragile direction,

don't look back with regretful reflection.

Other times other places,

down through lives with different faces.

Proceeding through time wearing a kaleidoscope of colors,

we change our minds and tolerance of others.

First, we're in then we're out,

questioning what each life's about.

Moving along to learn what we can be

we open our eyes so we can see.

With surprise we learn that others have memories of a different me.

What brings us through from dark to light,

until we are aware we finally got it right?

After passing along from life to life

we arrive at a blissful place hidden from sight.

Toni G. Robert

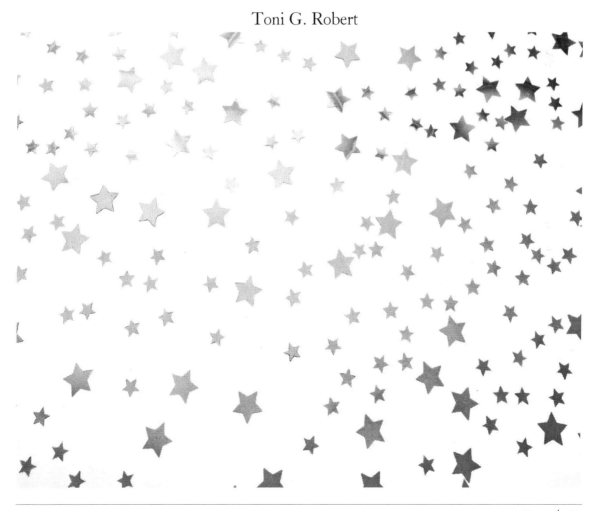

THE OPPORTUNITY OF A LIFETIME

Ships Log:

Today is August 21, 2018. I find myself in a slightly agitated, fully excited state. You'd think I'd be better composed, what with my extended experience in my chosen profession. But, today is different. Let me explain:

I am just a transplanted Jersey Girl. I have travelled the United States from Florida to Maine, New Jersey to California. I have been to Pennsylvania, Ohio, Illinois, Indiana, Michigan, Wisconsin, Delaware, Maryland, District of Columbia, Virginia, North and South Carolina, Georgia, Alabama, Tennessee, Connecticut, Massachusetts, Rhode Island, Vermont, Kansas, Nevada, Colorado, New Mexico, Texas, Quebec and Ontario and Mexico – but, never off of North America!

I never would have imagined being aboard the USS Gutenberg about to survey our vast solar system to provide us with a poetic journey of our nearby neighbors that are just beyond our atmosphere.

I am familiar with describing the beauty of waves crashing against the shores of the Atlantic and Pacific Oceans, feeling the cresting and ebb and flows while deep sea fishing for seabass and flounder off the Jersey shore, tasting and smelling the salt, and catching a sea breeze.

I am familiar with the beauty of nature I have witnessed in the Scenic Overlook near Bedminister, NJ where I stopped to make a written observation and named it "Stop and Smell the Roses."

I have observed the great Niagara Falls, watching the Maid of the Mist bounce in the foamy waters below as the waters roared above, shrouded in raingear attempting to stay dry to no avail, showered in beauty and majesty.

I have made my observations as I travelled down the Shenandoah Valley through the Appalachian Mountains, through the Tennessee Valley over hills and dales to make Alabama my new home base. Or how about when I got to view and live in the beautiful Rocky Mountains of Colorado with Pike's Peak of my morning backdrop, beautifully glistening with its remaining snowcap – or cross country skiing in Aspen and Vale – edges away from cliffs where million dollar homes stand perched on the sides of these majestic rocks.

I have written about birds, trees, flowers, forest creatures, insects, wind and clouds in vivid detail – making others hear the sounds, smell the fragrances, feel the breeze, see the rainbow of color dance across the page.

Now new visions of sights never before seen await me on my new assignment – Planet Mercury. In my effort to be properly informed, this is what I have learned so far about Mercury:

- It has no rings or moon.
- Its axis is tilted in such a way that there are no seasons.
- It takes 87 days to rotate around the sun.
- One day on Mercury is a total of 59 Earth days.
- It is full of craters, looking much like Earth's moon.
- Its surface has a layer of crust and a mantle which is both solid and brittle.
- Its core is molten or liquid.
- It is a terrestrial planet much like earth. It is 70% metallic; 30% silicate, and 42% iron, whereas our Earth is only 17% iron.
- Mercury is the closest to the Sun making it uninhabitable on that side and frigidly cold on the other side.

- The Caloris Basin is its largest feature caused by a meteorite crashing the surface millions of years ago leaving a 960. The Rachmaninoff Basin is 190 miles in diameter.

- There are cliffs hundreds of miles long and up to a mile high.

- It has no atmosphere, but it has an exosphere which is made up of oxygen, sodium, helium, hydrogen, and potassium.

- Water and ice exist in its polar region, leaving the perception that it is a barren planet.

- Mercury has a history of volcanic activity which resulted in the plains and smooth surfaces caused by lava flows but is now geologically inactive.

- It is the smallest planet. It would take 18 Mercuries to be the same size as Earth.

- Mercury was named after the Roman god of commerce, travel, thievery, and the Greek god Hermes, The Messenger of the gods because of his speed across the sky.

- Many of its craters, basins, et cetera have been named after famous artists, writers, musicians.

- The Mariner 10 was the first to visit Mercury 1974-1975.

- The Messenger did a fly by in 2008 and 2009.

- The Messenger began to further its study of the planet in 2011.

- The color of Mercury appears to be a dark gray mixed with lighter gray but would appear a grayish brown to the human eye.

- Mercury is 480, 319, 931 miles from Earth.

- Mercury is weightless. A human weighing 150 lbs. would weigh 87 lbs. on

Mercury – That's a good reason for me to move to Mercury, ummmm!

Our Mission should we chose to accept it:

- Bring back new information about the effects spending time on Mercury could have on our bodies, feelings, thinking, et. cetera through lab experiments.
- How we adapt to extreme heat and cold, living in darkness, and how it affects our anxiety and coping mechanisms.
- How we will get along in confined spaces.
- How our minds will calculate and process the unfamiliar sights we are bound to observe with all their nuances and mystery.

My part in this mission:

To find the words to describe something I have never before seen, felt, heard, or touched, will be my biggest challenge and/or obstacle by stretching by imagination farther than ever. I am, however, confident that I can meet the challenge, and bring you along for the ride of my life through the stars and galaxies.

First stop, MERCURY!

Patricia Woolfork

Summer 2018

We always look forward to spring break. In March of this year, my daughter went to Indiana. Of all things, I do not travel north in the wintertime. School break is fascinating because I keep three of my grandsons, but they spent that week with their dad. Their parents are divorced and their father had his leg amputated due to a sore on his foot. He kicked a toy which they had the floor covered with, which they often do if you don't keep after them for it. This sore got infected and set up blood poisoning. He had a couple of surgeries and tried to save the foot, but eventually lost his leg just below the knee. He was recuperating and not able to work, so they spent the week with him. My daughter said that she was going to northern Indiana to see her older sister and even if she had to go alone, she was going. So, I decided that I was going to go with her.

My daughter and I both crochet, so we took it along and, in the evenings, after she got off work we would all sit in the living room and crochet and visit with one another. On that Tuesday, my sister which I like to stay with in Nappanee, Indiana, and all of her daughters and daughters-in-laws came in and did spring cleaning for her. So, I didn't get to go and see her until Wednesday and spent the night with her. We had a good visit, and when my daughter came to pick me up, she took us across the street to see another one of our sisters who is three and a half years younger than I am. She had a bad stroke several years ago, which left her in a wheelchair with very limited speaking abilities. Her husband is retired, so he is able to be home and he takes good care of her. We couldn't be there any longer than an hour or so, as it tired her out very quickly. On our way back to Shipshewana where my daughter lives, we stopped and the E&S grocery store and did a little shopping. It's an "Amish" store, so it has no electricity and has thousands of items you can buy in bulk. We also stopped in to drop off a scrapbook my daughter updated for the man who restores baby grand pianos, from whom my daughter purchased one for herself. He is letting her do the sanding and painting on it at a discounted price.

Thursday evening, my brother and two sisters-in-law, niece, my two daughters, and I went out to eat at a little town named Ligonier for a fish dinner. Ligonier just happens to be famous for the marshmallows we purchase in the stores. They have a marshmallow festival every year. They have beautiful murals painted on the side of the buildings in town. On two of those buildings they have a train painted that actually "follows" you as you drive along and is facing you the entire time. It was very fascinating and exciting.

Going to Indiana we saw quite a bit of snow on the ground south of Indianapolis, but nothing in northern Indiana or Michigan. It was cold but very pretty, and we started for home on Saturday. We decided to do one more stop in Indiana, found a cute scrapbooking store that had card classes and had them displayed. They were all so pretty. Heartfelt Creations. My daughter searched them on the internet when we got back home and found out they were made right there in Goshen, Indiana where we had visited! We had a very nice time on our trip.

This same daughter and I left for Stewartsville, Alabama on Thursday morning of May 24th for a four-day church camp meeting. We had a wonderful time through May 27th. It reminded me of August 11, 1973 which was when we found the Church of God.

I also have a small raised garden at home. I grow lettuce, radishes, okra, tomatoes, eggplant, butter peas, and jalapenos. It always makes it better to have a few fresh vegetables from your own backyard. Friends are sharing green beans, cucumbers, squash, and sweet corn with us. It sure makes life sweet.

I love to work on quilts. I have finished a Cathedral window quilt which I've worked on for three and a half years. And I have a block of Sunbonnet Sue I'm working on when I go to the University Baptist Quilters group or to the Senior Center. And I am also working on a strip quilt at home. You sew two in strips, different colors or prints, on a nine-and-a-half-inch square and put together with strips in front and bias tape on the back. When they're all sewed and put together it doesn't need to be quilted. These are donations to the local fire stations and are given to people in need at Christmas time.

Our next expedition was going to the family reunion in Nappanee, Indiana on Labor Day weekend at a nephew's house. We usually have a hundred or more people come in for this event we celebrate about every two years. We have a very good time and get to see some family that we don't see very often from Florida, Georgia, Mississippi, Alabama, Pennsylvania, Colorado, Michigan, Kansas, Ohio, and Indiana. I can't remember where everyone comes from, but there are many.

My great granddaughter is getting married in October of this year in Chambersburg, Pennsylvania. I hope I get to go. She is the first great grandchild of over fifty to mine to get married. She has been on three mission trips with other young people from her church. The first trip was ten days in the Dominican Republic in February 2016. The group is called Team Partners. They helped with construction with churches and also helped with a school. Her longest mission trip was September 2016 to the end of April 2017. She lived in Guatemala for seven months. This last February she and her grandmother went to Haiti for two weeks. She is quite ambitious for a young girl.

September 16-21 is the church camp-meeting in Knoxville, Tennessee. I always look forward to going. We usually stay in a woman's dorm with women from Oklahoma, Florida, Alabama and other various places. We share a big room with beds for everyone and a place to hang our clothes and it is air conditioned. For the tabernacle they have a large tent they rent every year that holds right at two-hundred people and by Thursday night it is always full, with people even sitting outside on lawn chairs. The have two services a day, one in the morning and one in the evening. Breakfast is served from 7-8 am every morning, with prayer meetings a 9 am. Lunch is usually from 1-2 pm and dinner is served after the evening service at 6 pm. Young people services is at 2:30 pm and children services at 2 pm. On Thursday night, the children put on a program with lots of singing and skits or little plays for us and then they get a treat from the snack stand afterwards. The young people all go out to CiCi's Pizza on Thursday night for fellowship. On Saturday morning the local Knoxville congregation holds a picnic at a local park for all who want to come and serve pizza and play volleyball or ride bikes or any other games they have. It is an exciting time for all who attend. Seeing friends from Oklahoma, Ohio, Florida, and North Carolina is always a refreshing time for all.

On Thanksgiving we often have a family reunion just from myself down. My husband, my children's daddy, died of cancer in 1980. We number right now at one hundred. My daughter in Hartselle, Alabama used to have our family gatherings in her home, but we have outgrown it. So now we meet at a firehouse in Massey, Alabama which is very big and nice and can accommodate us all. It has a large place for the children to play and everyone is happy. There's a large kitchen and we all bring food to share and we all have a very good time.

Elizabeth Brown

My Little Radio

I looked up, what?

Ten 'til ten, Latin music plays

Slow Jazz beside me on the table.

My little radio

The size of the end of a bread box.

This radio's been dropped

Ninety-nine times, still plays.

No distinguishing dials to adjust

Just knobs,

Which knob do I turn?

One on each side.

Let me guess

This one, no this one, oh well

It's plugged up, so it's on.

It's no Sansui, like the one we desired

when we were young.

My little radio

Had longer than my last three pairs of

shoes.

Maybe it's a Tyqudo

No just an Acme.

My little radio will wake me up

Set for six am

It's 3 am, oh well.

Yank the cord, make coffee, wake up.

Plug the radio up.

Powers on

Plays music

Tells time.

With me when I'm lonely.

9 am a poem is read

Do good work

Keep in touch.

Drop the radio.

Rick Dowell

The Honor Box

On most weekday mornings, Jerry Lankford could be found at the American Legion Post at 2900 Drake Avenue S.W., sitting in one of the high, padded chairs at the end of the bar in the social quarters, drinking his coffee and checking for messages or making calls to members of the Post Honor Guard.

An Honor Guard member for over thirty years and Commander of Post 237's Honor Guard for more than twenty-three of those, Jerry was familiar with just about every patron of the organization and the stories behind most of the regular customers of the establishment.

Few of those stories were shared, if any, with others; the stories he loved to tell were of his travels to see his daughter in Florida or tales of the humorous happenings he had experienced on details with the Honor Guard volunteers; like the one involving the nicely dressed woman in high heels on a rainy day as the family laid a loved one to rest in a heavy downpour that left the gravesite surrounded by mud.

Though the matching umbrella protected her black dress, it did nothing for her shoes at the end of the service as she hurried to the shelter of her car, leaving one of them trapped in the reddish quicksand of the Alabama clay, and a nylon clad foot exposed to the unsympathetic ground of the cemetery that seemed to be trying to pull her into an early plot of her own.

The route she had chosen was also the one the Honor Guard had embarked on after the command, "Left face, half-step, march," and holding their weapons at Port Arms, the Commander and the Squad faced the same perilous path. But unlike the lady in distress, they were not dressed in heels and their heavy boots were in no danger of being sucked into the Netherworld or being sent to Post Everlasting.

And as any Southern gentleman would do, the Honor Guard Commander retrieved the shoe for the young woman, at the cost of his striped, uniform trousers becoming splattered with mud as the stubborn ground held onto its black, shiny prize, finally letting go with a sudden release that sent Jerry backward into the halted members of the rifle bearing squad lined up like dominoes behind him.

The shoe retrieved, and balance restored, the team slogged their way to the waiting van, amazed at just how much mud their boots could hold and how heavy they could become!

Though the rain had stopped upon their return to the Post, the heavy clumps of clay on their feet required removal before being allowed to enter the building and each of the Honor Guard members took turns with an outside water hose attached to a faucet; ensuring their humility, which was often threatened by their status as an elite, uniformed team.

There were other stories Jerry would tell, each one embellished with his unique style and magnetic charm; two things that had served him well as he searched for and recruited new members to an ever-changing roster.

A sense humor was essential in such an important duty as paying honor and respect to fallen veterans and comforting the families they left behind, for without it one could not go on without succumbing to the grief they witnessed repeatedly. Week after week–at one time reaching 300 details in a single year–the Honor Guard of Post 237 responded to the calls for graveside services, memorials, flag raisings, flag disposal ceremonies and parades in its service to the community.

Master storyteller that he was, Jerry Lankford also took his duty seriously— as one patron of the Post discovered when he picked up a copy of the *Old Huntsville Magazine* from the rack in the social quarters behind the seat Jerry occupied that day. Apparently unable to read the sign, the coin box and the price on the cover of the publication, and oblivious to the watchful eyes of the man drinking his morning coffee behind him, the man took the issue to a table and sat down to read—or look at the pictures in the publication.

Not until Jerry Lankford appeared at his side did he look up. "What?" he asked, defiantly.

"I know you saw the sign that said 75 cents," Jerry said. "You know, when you take that magazine without paying for it, you are stealing money from kids in hospitals and that is about the lowest thing anyone could do. Now, either put that back or put the money in the box."

The man looked at Jerry, "You're kidding, right? You would dress me down over a paper? I'll put it back after I read it," the man said, "I don't have any change."

"You'll put it back now or I'll put it back after I put you outside," Jerry said.

Regarding Jerry's tone of voice and the look in his eyes, the man chose the wiser path of nodding and saying, "Okay," as he stood up and walked to the stand to replace the purloined issue.

Satisfied, Jerry returned to his now lukewarm coffee and held it up for the bartender's attention.

As she returned with a fresh cup, she motioned to Jerry with her eyes. Turning around in his chair he watched as the man struggled to put a rolled-up $5.00 bill into the slot of the coin box, finally succeeding.

The Honor Guard Commander turned back around, winked at the bartender, and smiled as took the waiting cup and filed the incident for a future story to tell.

John E. Carson

Balloons Float Up

Balloons float up

Rain falls down.

Grass is green

Then it's brown.

The flowers bloom

Then they die.

Bees make honey

Don't know why.

Waves keep crashing

From the sea.

Someone's in charge

It isn't me.

Betty Pettigrew

The Battle of Huntsville

Terror gripped Huntsville as the horrible message spread throughout the community: "The Indians are coming! They're killing everyone!"

Men, women, and children, determined not to risk their fate at the hands of the bloodthirsty savages, began fleeing their homes. Within hours, the only people left to defend Huntsville from the impending doom were five courageous men who had barricaded themselves in the new courthouse. The year was 1813 and North Alabama was plagued by marauding bands of Creek Indians. The battle of Fort Mims had recently taken place, with Indians killing hundreds of settlers. Reports of hideous massacres, scalping, and other atrocities spread like wildfire with every passing stranger.

Huntsville's population was about 1,500 souls, of whom 250 were slaves. The town, in its few short years, had already become a prosperous and thriving community. On the grounds around the courthouse, which was the town center, people would gather under the big, sprawling oak trees to buy and sell cotton, swap tales, and quiz passing strangers about news from other towns.

The first word of the approaching Indians came from a thirsty traveler who had stopped to water his horse. The citizens gathered as he told of savage warriors he had seen on his journey. One local gent passed the stranger a jug of spirits. The news of the Indians seemed to become even more ferocious as the jug made its rounds from man to man. The stranger spoke of being chased to the very edge of town by the red men. You could have heard a pin drop on the old courthouse square that day as the townspeople clung to his every word. Gradually the crowd dispersed, with worried men pondering the best ways to protect their families. When a few men put their women and children in carriages for the journey north and out of harm's way, the panic began. Farmers left their tools lying in the fields, women left their food still hot on the stoves, everyone was trying to flee Huntsville as fast as they could.

Masters and slaves alike competed for any kind of transportation they could find. With the exodus north, plantations were abandoned, and families separated as the cry became "every man for himself".

In a few short hours, Huntsville had become a ghost town.

Meanwhile the famous Indian fighter, Andrew Jackson, who was camped 25 miles away at Fayetteville, Tennessee, had received word of the impending massacre. Rallying his troops, he ordered a nonstop march all the way to Huntsville, without rest or food. He reminded the soldiers of all the helpless families that would surely be lolled if the army did not reach Huntsville in time.

As the soldiers marched south to save Huntsville, the frightened populace continued its scramble north. Gloom settled over the town as it became abandoned, with no one left to defend it.

No one, that is, except for five brave men who barricaded themselves in the new brick courthouse, determined to defend to the death the town they had helped to carve out of the wilderness.

Captain Wyatt was no stranger to fighting Indians. He assumed command of the brave little group in the courthouse that day, knowing the odds were against him. But if he could delay the Indians, perhaps Andrew Jackson would arrive with his troops in time to save the day. Rumor had it that even Davy Crockett was headed toward Huntsville with his long rifle, determined to whip the red rascals once and for all!

It was a long, dark night as they paced to and fro in the courthouse, peering often out the windows. Capt. Wyatt, in an attempt to bolster his men's sagging morale, passed around a jug of whiskey, and then another ... and another.

Finally, with nerves at the breaking point, a shadow was seen darting behind the bushes in the courthouse yard. A shout rang out: "Indians, the Indians are here!" Men rushed to their posts and began firing.

The battle of Huntsville was on.

Gunshots rang out through the night as the stalwart defenders fired, reloaded and fired again, pausing only long enough to wipe the powder stains from their tired faces and to take another drink.

As the sun rose over Huntsville that next morning, it revealed a scene of utter devastation. All around the courthouse square, windows lay shattered, doors were shot off their hinges, and the acrid smell of gunpowder hung heavily in the air.

Gen. Andrew Jackson and Davy Crockett marched slowly into town at the head of the brave Tennessee volunteers. With guns primed and loaded, the soldiers slowly fanned out across the square. Veterans of a hundred Indian battles, they were amazed and at the same time terrified at the devastation the night's battle had wrought.

The great battle fought in Huntsville that night might have gone down in history books except for one small detail.

There were no Indians!

The brave courageous defenders of our fair city had been firing at shadows.

The stranger who had first spread the story of the Indians had long disappeared and the only hostile Indians within a hundred miles were those visions that emerged from the whiskey jugs.

Today, where Holmes Avenue intersects with Lincoln Street, one will see a historical marker that tells how Gen. Jackson and Davy Crockett camped there after a long, hard march from Tennessee. The marker does not tell why they came here.

Now you know.

Tom Carney

The Final Frontier

A	B	C	D	E	F	G	H	I	J	K	L	M	N	O	P	Q	R	S	T	U	V	W	X	Y	Z
							4							16											

H _ _ _ _   _ _ _   H _ _   O _ _ _ _ _ _   O _ _   H _ _
17 4 12 20 12   3 5 12   17 4 12   2 16 8 3 9 12 20   16 25   17 4 12

_ _ H _ _ _ _ _   _ _ _ _ _ _ _ _ _ .
20 17 3 5 20 4 13 22   9 18 17 12 23 7 12 5 9

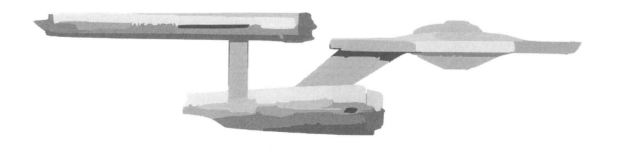

My Own Path to Real True Love, then...The Rest of the Story

The title of this story reminds me of the late television and radio man Paul Harvey and his feel-good noontime stories with two happy endings. The first happy ending came almost at the end of the story only to be followed up with a jaw dropping ending know to all as "the rest of the story". If you enjoyed Paul Harvey's *The Rest of the Story,* this story may be for you and yours.

***

It was October 19th, 1978, the afternoon of our wedding and honeymoon, which took place at Montgomery Bell State Park just west of Nashville, Tennessee. My new bride Rita Kaye, a PhD and University professor, and her two small dogs and myself were laying by the small den fireplace. We were watching the flames dance around while we began planning our future together. Rita Kaye was, I am sure, sent by God to complete me as a person. Rita was to me the smartest person I had ever known. Rita had everything at thirty years old, but unknown to me her doctors had told her that she had the bones of a seventy or eighty-year-old woman. But to me she had great skin that covered them all up. Sure, she hid this from me, fearing that I would not marry her, but that would have made no difference. Because when I looked at Rita's body, the three ruptured discs and bad bones were well covered up by some wonderful skin and a lot of other good stuff. In fact, with a bad back she still beat me in a game of tennis that afternoon, I remembered as we lay on the floor near the fireplace. I was like a man in the Apple Store for the very first time. Rita had a super high IQ and a killer body. It was just like when the new Apple iPhone 7 first came out. I could ask her any question I wanted to and there was a 99.9% chance she would tell me what I needed or wanted to know. The biggest thing I will never understand is why Rita ever asked me to marry her. She at every turn refused to take no for an answer. I would point out all of my weak points and she would point out all of my strong points. Then in Rita Kaye's mind when she met my family and father, that was it. Rita Kaye loved my father to death because he would kid around with her and make her smile. Until the day we married and all the days after that I promised that I would always love her and be kind to her. I said to myself as we lay by the fire that afternoon when I asked this question. As the teacher in Rita Kaye kicked in, I asked her the first big question that would change my life forever.

I said, "Rita, I want to be the best husband possible," (and I would read every self-help book I could get my hands on). "Rita, what is the best way to build a habit of any kind?" She smiled and kissed me on the tip of my nose and began to teach me.

She said, "It's simple, all you have to do is repeat the same act for twenty-two days in a row. It has been proven in studies that you will develop a habit. But the studies also show that if you miss even one day you must start all over again."

Perhaps because we were in our honeymoon phase, I prayer: *Dear God, please let me do an act of kindness every day we are together until death do us part.* (Then as an afterthought I asked *please God let me do really big acts of kindness and not any small acts.*) I never told Rita Kaye about my prayer because if I failed I did not want it thrown back in my face for the rest of my life.

I did do what I prayed I wanted to do. I remember counting through twenty-seven days until I forgot to count, and I created a new habit. But each day, no matter what, I would do really big acts of kindness for almost thirty years. Now, what happened next is the rest of the story:

Part II: The Rest of the Story

Someone once asked the great movie star Cary Grant, born Archie Leach, at the end of his long career to tell the readers just how he became Cary Grant. "I pretended to be somebody I wanted to be and I finally became that person. Or he became me. Or we met at some point." This statement said to me that for every twenty-two days or longer in a row that Cary Grant reinstated or made a new habit, good or bad, all together made him, forty years later, the man millions knew and love.

***

Now let's leap ahead thirty years to October 19th, 2008 to see what happened when I was reminded for the first time that I ever prayed that honeymoon prayer. My wife Rita Kaye had been in bed for weeks due to the pain that ran all through her sixty-year-old body. It was about 9 AM and I had been to the place where Rita loved to eat breakfast to buy three big deluxe breakfasts with an order of pancakes on the side. Two of the three breakfasts were for me. Rita Kaye was very upset because she did not know where I had been for what seemed like hours to her. Brody was our sixteen-year-old foster son who had been living in our home for the past year. He moved in when we were told that he had no other place in the state of Alabama to go. No one who would take the risk they thought he was to others and they didn't feel safe enough to have him in their home or group homes. So until Brody was nineteen-years-old the powers that be okayed him living with us. Deep down Brody was an eleven-year-old living in a sixteen-year-old body. He was the most self-centered person I had ever known. Brody kept his true feelings buried very, very deep.

I put my breakfast down on the table with Brody's, and the other one I gave to Brody to take to Rita Kaye's bedside. Rita Kaye was really mad at me for being gone so long. She lashed out at me because of the sharp pain she was in. Brody really loved Rita because she gave him anything he ever asked for. For the most part he always sided with Rita no matter what. Brody sat down near Rita's bed, and to my shock, started taking up for me.

"Now Rita", he said, "just hold up please." Brody looked up at me standing up then looked back down at Rita. "I have been living here every day this entire year. I have been watching Harold Lee. I have noted that every day that I have lived here that he does something really kind for you. Every day I am talking about." (The next words out of his mouth were the exact words I used in my honeymoon prayer thirty years before, words that had not even crossed my mind since then. I even forgot them since the twenty-seventh day of build a healthy habit, plus my words were only for my silent lips to God's ears and no one else.) Then Brody went on with these words. "Harold Lee every day does something really, really kind for you. Every day. And not just small kind things either. I am talking about really, really big things."

My jaw dropped open and I felt God's presence among us. There was silence and a smile came to Rita's lips and her face lit up. After a minute or two I asked Brody to go eat his breakfast before it got cold because Rita and I really needed to have a heart to heart talk. Rita, for the first time in a long time, acted grateful for all the acts of kindness I had ever done for her. She also told me she would never take me for granted again.

Rita also wanted to do something nice for Brody for opening up her eyes. "I think I will run by Brody's foster care supervisors the idea of the three of us to go up somewhere around Ashville, North Carolina to vacation with Brody's mother." She was doing well now since Brody and his two brothers were taken away from her when

Brody was around eleven years old. Neither I, nor Rita Vest would have been able to make this happen but for Rita Vest, Ph.D., anything was possible. And just like all of our affairs, she was like a super computer and made everything come together. We took Brody to a nearby Days Inn, close to Brody's grandmother's house. Brody's mother and two brothers came by the Days Inn and Brody left with them. Every two days or so they would bring food and photos for the two of us to see. At the end of the week we spent the entire day with everyone at Brody's grandmother. The night before we were to end our visit/vacation I asked Rita this important question.

"Rita, I want you and I to pray before we go to sleep and again first thing in the morning to ask God's help in getting Brody back in our car and back in foster care in Alabama."

"That sounds good, Harold Lee, and while we are on the subject, there's one more thing I need to tell you, just in case," Rita replied.

"What's that Rita Kaye?"

"Well, dear, it's like this. I never asked Alabama foster care for permission to let Brody go off and stay away from us to that he could have as much time here with them as possible."

"Rita Kaye?" I had never let that run through my mind.

We slept in the next morning knowing that for this deed we might earn us a small home in Heaven. Before we knew it there was a bang on the front door. Bang! Bang! Bang! "Wake up you guys!"

I opened the door. There was Brody and his entire family. They wanted to leave early and spend time in the Tennessee mountains with us. Rita and I hugged Brody and were both so happy that God had blessed us again.

Harold Lee Vest

The Midnight Tree

Come boys and girls and listen to me and I shall tell of the Midnight tree. One frosty night we did attest to do our very, very best to find the one most perfect tree for Santa and his elves to see. We rode in a sleigh both far and wide to search out all the country side, until we saw one mountain high the moon shown through the midnight sky. The glistening branches filled like stars with icicles beaming from its boughs. I knew that Santa would agree the Midnight tree was made for me. It shook its branches like tinkling bells this moon lit night and I could see an angel appear on the top of that tree. The deer and elk stood watch in wait as we cut down and wrapped this tree to take.

We placed it in the window wide and decorated it with loving pride. Candy canes and little trains and popcorn and cranberry and tinsel exclaimed a Merry Christmas for all to see on this Midnight perfect Christmas tree.

The moon showed through the window pane. It's Santa and reindeer I did proclaim! A, "ho-ho-ho." I heard from the roof and many little reindeer hoofs. I hid in the curtains so he could not see I wasn't in the bed as I ought to be. After placing the presents I heard him say, "The most beautiful tree I've seen today."

Carol Wells Barnette

The Treasure

I saw it first, then she said, "Let's grab it before the others do." We did.

Little did we know that day would be relived over-and-over again for the rest of our lives. We were born different years, but only a few months apart. Uncle Herbert, her daddy, and my mama, shared the same mom and dad, we knew them as Mama and Papa.

Sarah Ann (the only red head) and I were best buddies growing up, best cousin buddies.

Christmas and a summer picnic were the only times that all twenty-eight grandkids were together. Most Sunday afternoons were spent at Mama and Papa's house but not this particular day. Sarah Ann's house was in the country and had a screened-in front porch. There was a weathered barn and beside it there was a thicket of tall pine trees.

After lunch we anxiously awaited the homemade ice cream. Two faded green wooden churns, hand-cranked (by the men) were slowly turning the secret ingredients that would produce our long-anticipated brain freezes; nonetheless, it would be worth it. As the ice cream began to harden, the churning and turning took more muscle. One of the uncles would call for some of us kids to help by sitting on top of the churn, to steady it. Several layers of old newspapers were doubled-over and placed on top of the churn. Our bottoms still got chilled.

That day, Sarah Ann and I decided to let some of the younger kids help with the ice cream. Somehow, we managed to be alone, which wasn't easy with that many cousins around.

That's when I spotted it. Had it dropped off of a truck? Did someone lose it? Could this really be happening to us? Then she saw it! I looked at her and we both ran to the road to capture it. It probably had been cut the day before, but seemed to be okay, except for a little mud. We knew that we had happened upon a treasure.

Should we tell? The right thing was to share. Did it belong to someone else? We knew it wasn't ours. What should we do?

Squealing from the backside of the house was getting closer, closer...

"Run, for your life!" I elbowed Sarah Ann.

They spotted us and the chase was on. We were older, faster and much wiser, at the ripe old age of nine. Darting in-and-out of the pine trees, we suddenly slipped on the pine straw. We were down and that's when it hit us, "Cover each other in pine straw, they'll never notice us." It worked and we were not discovered.

Knowing the best escape route, I let Sarah Ann lead, as she was in familiar territory. Sneaking slowly to the back of the barn then up the hidden ladder, we reached the loft. We would be safe there; she, me and our *treasure*.

Now we were both raised to share and never waste, but I knew that we couldn't share, not this time. There wasn't enough for everyone, way too many cousins. Anyway, they could have our share of the ice cream.

As luck would have it, we spotted an old rusted knife, and dull as it was, it served our purpose. We had eaten sugarcane before, that's how we knew how special it was. Cutting and stripping the outer layer off the stalk will get you to the good stuff. Only eat the inside, but you actually don't eat it, just chew it. (Sort of like cows, chewing their cud). When the sweet is gone, you just spit it out, grab another chunk of stalk and start over again. It took us about an hour and we didn't waste one bite.

Yep! The two of us did what any clever 9-year-old cousin-best-buddies would do, we ate it by ourselves. We ate it all.

We put the knife back and plucked pine needles from each other's hair. Nonchalantly walking into the back yard, we noticed that the rock salt and half melted ice had been tossed into the side yard. The aunts were inside washing the glass bowls (no plastic or paper back then).

Two of our uncles were leaned back on the oak tree, in their cane-bottom chairs. They would spin their tales of younger days (as men-folk do). The ice cream paddles were clean, that was okay because we had our very own "secret-happy." Some of the little kids had fallen asleep in the shade on some family made quilts.

It didn't take long until one of the uncles said, "Gather up the young'uns, it's time to head to the house."

That started the process of loading the cars, finding the dishes you had brought, finding the kids, hugs good-bye, one last dash to the potty, finding the kids again; and one car was away.

I begged to spend the night with Sarah Ann, as best buddy cousins, we always begged to stay together, sometimes we even shed tears. Sometimes it worked, sometimes it didn't. This time it did.

We waved and hugged our families farewell. Sticking out our tongues, me and Sarah Ann, teased the *other* cousins. They weren't as *lucky* as us, our adventures were to continue and *they* had to go home.

Sundown came quickly and that was fine, we were ready for bed. Feeling a little yucky in our tummy, things weren't going like we had planned and in no time at all, we were both sick, heaving up *our treasure* and hugging the commode.

Sarah Ann's momma took care of us; as best as she could.

Well, the *sick*, wouldn't stop. She finally asked us, "Just what did you two eat today?"

By that time, we didn't care about *our secret* we just wanted relief.

We told our sworn-to-silence secret.

Climbing the loft ladder, armed with a flashlight in hand, her dad, Uncle Herbert, found the remnants of *our treasure.*

Slightly smiling, Uncle Herbert presented the evidence to Aunt Martha and as I remember it, they both started laughing. Oh, they tried to disguise it, but I saw their snickers. Here are these two sweet and innocent little girls, gaging and heaving, (thinking they were dying) and *they* thought it was funny. That was not nice. Cruel is what it was.

The next day I went back home and she stayed home. Needless to say, we survived and memories were made. The story has been told and retold throughout both of our lives. We still laugh about that fateful day, as do the thankful-cousins that didn't get to share in *our treasure.*

Two 9-year-old best-buddy cousins learned a valuable lesson that summer.

Make sure you know what you are eating because…

sugarcane and corn stalk are not the same thing!

Belinda Talley

Leon the Lazy Angel

No one could understand it
Why Leon was always late
He couldn't help being lazy
"It must just be my fate!"

When it came time to sing His praises
Leon was always last
Still sound asleep 'til
Gabriel's horn would blast.

Then Leon would jump
Awaking with a start
Rolling off his cloud
And clutching at his heart.

A blaze of flickering light
His halo all askew
Still in his pajama robe
The little angel flew.

Just in time he took his place
As the bells began the ring
And just in time he cleared his throat
As the choir began to sing.

Now, Gabriel was patient
As most angels are
Though there were times he wanted
To turn Leon into a star!

Still, no one was anxious
To take the matter to God
So every now and then
They'd give him a little prod.
After all, he WAS an angel

And perfect they were inside
Their record was impeccable
Almost a matter of pride!

So every day the trumpet sound
Woke them from their rest
Each shift of the choir
Would go and sing their best.
One day the Heavenly News
Announced the coming Birth
And certain angels were call to Earth.

When Gabriel saw the list
He dreaded and feared the worst
Leon had been chosen
To tell the shepherds first!

Now he wished he would have
Told God of Leon's test
On this Most Important Day
God thought Leon best?

Gabriel paced forth and back
Beside the crystal lake
How could he save the day
What direction should he take?

Then came inspiration
Came from out of the blue
And picking up his horn
He knew exactly what to do!

When Leon saw the list
His heart started to pound

"Oh wow, oh now I must not miss
Gabriel's trumpet sound!"

So nervous was Leon
The night before the Birth
That he couldn't sleep a wink
Thinking of the Earth.

Some time before midnight
He drifted off to sleep
He had prayed and prayed to God
His wake up time to keep.

Gabriel flew silent
Over Leon's cloud
He stopped and tuned his trumpet
Extra long and loud.

The other angels rested
Waiting for their time
Some had already started
To find their place in line.

Then Gabriel gave the sounding blast
But not an angel stirred
He had tuned his trumpet
So only Leon heard!

The first blast didn't wake him
But the second one sure did
Leon rolled off his cloud

His sleepy wings still hid!

"Oh my gosh! I'm so late!"
Was all that he could say
As he dashed off to Bethlehem
On this Most Important Day!

As he reached his station
Under the blazing star
He saw no other angels
Either near or far!

"I must have missed the whole thing—
Whatever will I do?
God will not be happy
Nor will Gabriel too!"

Then he saw the shepherds
Still keeping their sheep
And began to tell the news
While they lay fast asleep.

As the shepherds woke one by one
The other angels came
And Leon knew what had happened
And felt a twinge of shame.

But God knew what he was doing
So everything turned out well
And Leon the Lazy Angel
Became the First Noel.

John Evan Carson

Venus: The Love Shack

* Author's note: This is a chapter of an ongoing story. Since it isn't the beginning or the end, I will give you a little beginning so you won't be so confused.

The Government has built 8 space ships. One each going to a planet in our solar system. The Government wants to get rid of us because there are too many people. No one had a choice and we haven't inhabited the planets yet.

Group two that was supposed to go the planet Venus, had been scheduled that morning. They all had gotten on the ship, strapped in their seats, and when the large bubble came down over their heads, they waited nervously for the gas to put them in a hibernation like sleep. They waited and waited. No such gas was released. It was found that it wasn't working and it would be awhile before it could be fixed. They were instructed to go back to their building and wait. All 2500 of them.

They ended up waiting for a week before it was fixed. By then they had missed their window of lift off time and had to wait longer. Their classes were finished, so what would they do to wait? While they waited, they started hearing back stories of group one that had already reached their planet of Mercury. They got the stories back by satellite. One story was a bit hard to believe. It was about these two men that had gone outside when the Sun was going down. One of them had smuggled a flask of whiskey in one of his pockets. Just as he thought that the temperature would be bearable, he took a swig of the whiskey. Well, the whiskey that he had drank crystallized in his lungs and his throat and killed him immediately. The other man high tailed it right back to the ship. They had been warned not to take any food outside with them. That also included liquids as well.

When the people in group two destined for Venus heard this story, they worried all the more. They thought that Venus was hot all the time, a constant 863 degrees. What would food and drink do to them if eaten outside their ship?

While everyone was waiting, some of us became restless and just had to do something, other than just sit in our rooms. We went outside and would look up at the night sky trying to spot "our planet". A teenager all of a sudden exclaimed, "hey I can see my shadow! And the sun is down and the moon isn't shining!" A man says that is because the planet Venus is so bright. It goes around the Sun every 225 days, and when it is at the right place, it is at its brightest and can give you a shadow. It's the brightest thing in the sky next to the sun and our moon. We can even see Venus sometimes during the day.

Well it comes time for us to leave on our space ship. We get back on and lift off.

Soon, was your feeling, you are already waking up orbiting Venus. It may seem like just a short time, but you have traveled 38 million miles to get here. If you had left earth not during a window opening, you could have traveled up to 162 million miles to get here. That's how far Venus can travel away from earth in its orbit around the Sun and that happens every 584 days.

You look out a window and see...nothing. Well not nothing. You see clouds and lots of them. You could be looking at Earth, but then again, no. Not even Earth has so many clouds that you can't see some of the planet itself.

You look to the side of the clouds, out in space. You know that there are no moons here. There isn't any gravitational pull for moons. But what is it that you see?

Your orbiting closer to it. You finally get close enough to make out the word NASA on the side. You breathe some relief. Maybe we are in better hands than we thought. Hey, disappointed you realize there is no one there. It's just an unmanned space craft. You turn your attention back to Venus.

With the instruments that you were given, you can make out tall mountains. Some are measured up to 7 miles high. Wow! Many of the mountains are not just mountains, but volcanoes and very active.

You were told that sulfuric acid dominates the composition of the clouds. But studying it now at a closer view it looks much more complex than that. The winds seem to be outrageous. The clouds haven't been swept away and are constantly reforming to stay there.

You finally get samples and are totally confused. Some of the cloud samples are not sulfur at all but chlorine. A salt like your stomach acid.

There won't be running on this planet. Even if the temperature was mild. The terrain is too rough and rocky. You would be tripped up constantly.

You study the mountains. You certainly can't land the space ship there. Even the shuttle crafts are too big for the mountain's steep sides and pointy tops.

You figure out a way to sheer off the tops, big enough and flat enough for a shuttle craft.

One shuttle is sent down to test. Twenty people go in this trip. They land and draw lots to see who will go first. At three different times one person goes out. They don't come back. They have died, burned up. The seventeen that are left, take the shuttle back to the ship and report what happened.

Someone speaks up and says, "we are going to have to live on this planet somehow. The clothes that were given to us just won't work. We will have to adapt them to this world."

You try fashioning long ears to the head gear thinking that it may release some of your body heat. Then you think of the three that have already attempted walking on the planet. The report was they hurried. Well, what if you walked slowly and reserved your energy? Then last, have a constant flow of not cold but a few degrees cooler than body temperature flowing down your throat.

The next shuttle to go had another twenty people. They discovered that they would survive on short walks outside the shuttle. They all came back and reported.

The next update was to build a tunnel and make a cave at the end to live in. It took quite a while and many trips, but they finally accomplished this. They found that a strong closed door at the entrance to the tunnel would make the cave just livable. Many mountains are then set up with these tunnels and caves.

While this was going on, there were other groups of people with different challenges. One was to figure out how to create water and air. They finally were able to accomplish this by taking the three levels of cloud formations and the atmosphere close to the planet. By putting them together in such a way and with fire and ice, they succeeded.

Well we need air, for without air we can die within minutes. We need water, for without water our bodies can start to shut down between three and ten days. Now food, some people have gone twenty or more days without food. We had read about a strange man in history that did that, named Ghandi.

So, the other group was to find something edible on the planet and, or at least dirt that we will be able to grow our food in. They would walk very slowly down the steep sides of the mountain searching. At one time, a woman at a certain level discovered pock mark holes. Looking in one she saw a clear substance. Almost like water but very thick. Inside were fish like creatures. For they were swimming very slowly around. However, they had huge heads and small bodies unlike the fish back home that had small heads and large bodies. She thought "I wonder if we can eat them."

A man at another level discovered small foxlike creatures and mice. Only their ears were very long and stood straight up from their heads. They were smooth like satin and didn't have any hair on them. The rest of their bodies had a thick close-cropped hair; even their tails had this hair. They too had large heads and small bodies like the fish.

The people started to relax. They got their food. The fish, they called poc-fish, and when cooked properly, it didn't taste half bad. Almost like sardines. They didn't need to salt them for they were already very salty. The mice were pretty good too. Almost like chicken, but not. But the fox meat. It was very strong and tough. It was hard to choke down. They thought that it may be due to the fact that its urine was very thick and the fox didn't go to the bathroom but once a day. When thinking about that too much, it would make you choke all the more. They even tended to the nicely growing gardens and would soon have fresh vegetables.

There wasn't much else to do after working so hard all this time to just try and survive. So now the people were having sex. It was wondered in 9-10 months just how many babies would be born? There wasn't anything available to keep from getting pregnant. Maybe being on this planet was having an effect on them. After all this planet was Venus. The Goddess of love.

Margaret J. Forrest

THE CHRISTMAS PURSE

The Purse from God and Me

It's been over fifty years ago now, in December of 1967, when I was a young seventeen-year-old Baptist preacher. My Mama had only days to live before she joined Christ up above. We were poor, and I had only three dollars to my name. But I made my way to the Old Miller's discount department store in Birmingham, Alabama, having no idea of what I could buy. I prayed to God, asking him to lead me to the best gift that I could buy that would clearly send Mama a message of how much I loved her and that I wanted her to stay a little longer.

I looked over hundreds of things but nothing cried out to me as the perfect gift for me to buy with my three dollars. With my head hung down, something touched me, and I looked up and saw just what I needed to make the statement I wanted to make. It was a purse, and after taxes, left me with exactly three pennies.

That night, some of my family members who were looking on scoffed at my present, but the joke was on them. When Mama saw the purse, her face lit up and she smiled the biggest smile. That was the best gift she could have given back to me.

That smile still warms my heart. And I still have that three-dollar purse. I would not sell it for a million dollars, because God picked it out for me.

Harold Lee Vest

RETNIW NAM DLO

In my travels over the world, I have met many wise and amazing individuals. Four of my favorites live in an ancient stone castle in the Far North. In ages past the four were assigned the eternal task of creating the seasons for all the world. Each was given an equal portion of the year. Since the seasons are cyclical and different in other parts of the world, they are working through the year.

Retniw chose the location for their home because he is the most powerful of the four. The other three, Gnirps, Remmus and Llaf, have little to do compared to Retniw. The three seasons each of them design, although magnificent, are mild next to the season he controls.

Retniw controls the dramatic and powerful season of winter. He supervises the wind, snow, clouds and howls that he so carefully designs each year. Retniw orchestrates each part as if it was an instrument in a great symphony.

I most enjoy visiting Retniw in the fall, just as he is putting the last movements in the score for the coming season. This is the time when he most welcomes company from outside. He keeps his secrets well. Never will he tell me what he has planned for the next winter season. Nor will he confide in me as to the possibility for a White Christmas.

Sitting in the main room he works in is enough to warm my soul. The room is quite simple. The furnishings render the space cozy and warm. As late fall usually carries a chill, the bench in front of the fireplace provides a delightful place to seat myself. There are two benches in the room. They are of stick construction and adorned with a large white cushion stuffed with goose down, providing quite comfortable seating.

The floor is bare of rugs and the light pouring through the textured glass of the two large windows cast strange patterns on the wooden floor planks. The two windows cover a whole wall except for a two-foot space between them. The frames rise to the ceiling and begin at the top of the bench that is the length of the wall. The textured glass looks as if hundreds of wine bottles had given up their bottoms, then joined together the circles of glass to form the panes. Each window is surrounded by an arch with a ledge a foot deep. One window ledge features a human skull with the lower jaw missing.

The foot-thick walls are of plaster. The ceiling is exposed beam with decorative molding around the edge. Exposed posts are at each corner of the room and a large gourd with the stem and a leaf still attached, hangs from the ceiling.

On the same wall as the fireplace, twine is hung horizontally, attached every four inches or so. Scraps of paper and an old pair of scissors are stuffed in the twine for safe keeping. Bottles sitting high on a shelf over the mantel are filled with remedies and warm brew. A large brim hat with tassels attached to the band hangs nearby. A large hour glass hangs near the hat.

The rest of the room is scattered with few objects. Under the window bench is a small chest with an ornate gold latch. Next to the chest are a pair of brown slippers that look like they are made from leather. On the second window ledge are a few down pillows and ancient books.

Retniw's desk is like a four-legged animal standing with legs spread wide. A tabletop replaces the animal's body. Retniw sits from dawn to dusk at this desk, designing winter. He wears robes that resemble those of a monk and sports a long white beard and a pleasant look on his face. His eyes are like blue ice and only the sides of his head grow hair to match his beard. The top of his scalp is shiny and smooth.

Companionship during the year comes from a large white lion and a small white fox. They stay by his side at all times. Why the strange pair are there will always be a mystery to me. But, I do know Retniw Nam Dlo will visit my home this year as he always has.

Sandy Ballas

Voices echo up and down the cul-de-sac.
A woman in a big, yellow hat
takes her morning constitutional down
the winding paved road.
The crows are at their cawing again
sending code to one another.
The faint chirp of another bird is drowned out
by the cacophony made by the crows.
Their noise is punctuated by bark of a far off dog,
its peace constantly interrupted by
this constant conversation.

The houses almost disappear among the landscape.
They are colored like nature –
grays, browns, taupe, and
autumnal hues of orange and gold –
Brick, stucco, and wooden planks fit so effortlessly
behind the shade of the ever green pines,
the aspens and occasional willow.
Driveways are lined with stones and rocks, and the
yards accented with stoned walls and embankments.

WOOF, CAW, chirp, buzz, CAW, CAW,
WOOF, WOOF, WOOF small dog – yap!
The only other sound I hear in this magical place
is the scurrying the squirrel makes
going through the grass on its mission to reach a tree.

An occasional butterfly crosses my line of vision
– the jewel of radiant color –
that compliments the hanging baskets of begonias and
garden flora of pinks, reds, yellows, and oranges
that are visible across the road.

Tranquility is the word I'd use for this bath of beauty

I find myself luxuriating in this fine morning.
How can anyone truly believe
that this all happened by accident?
It is as though a very skilled artist
tipped his brush into his palette
and made broad strokes to create
the blue mixed with white to form the sky;
dabbed into the earth tones
to punctuate the horizon
with the peaks and valleys of the mountain range,
then decided to cap the tallest one
with just a touch of white
to make it just that much more majestic.
Then he colored the ground
with greens, reds, and browns
so that our eyes could be amazed
by the proliferation of color
making them able to jump from one color to the next
with the motion of a wave,
the ripple on the surface of the water
– rocking us gently –
in the arms of natural wonder.

Our senses cannot help but be awakened
in this mountainous paradise.
Sight, sound, smells, even taste,
are equally entertained.

The wind is still today.
The chimes on the porch barely move.
The flies have taken their turn today,
buzzing around me as I write.
I do hear the crickets though
as I watch a solitary ant weave back and forth
across the concrete porch
searching for a path back into the garden.

One might think the fly to be a pest, and
it really is, but
it serves a purpose also.
It interrupts my consciousness and
alerts me to the other sounds surrounding me
I may have overlooked without
the persistent annoyance of this singular pesky fly!

The sun is warm on my feet although
the rest of me is hidden in the shade.
I feel really alive!
My words cannot fully express
my wonderment and awe.
Yet, I try to convey
what my sight and senses tell me as
the wisp of a breeze caresses my ear,
tenderly kisses my neck,
and makes the chime sing again as if . . .
My Creator
UNDERSTANDS . . .
EVERYTHING . . .
I've written on this page!

July 8, 2015 - Monument, Colorado

Even the fog
Makes a glorious appearance
High up in these Rocky Mountains.
Like a bridal veil,
Its mist obscures the craggy beauty of the ridges
And adorns them in a glistening haze.

One wonders from this distance if
It is raining up on the Peak,
Or
  If snow
    Is falling
      Once again.

It has been unseasonably cold the past few days,
So it is a possibility.

I won't know
Which it is
Until I go outdoors, again,
Tomorrow
To see
What wonders
Await me.

    Patricia Woolfork

DRACULA

Around 1958 a lot of American movies came to Holland, some funny, some war stories, and one category was scary movies.

One day, my friend and I read that a Dracula movie was coming to town. I lived in the city of Gouda, in the Netherlands and this was big news.

It was said that this movie was really scary, different and something never shown in theaters here before. My friend and I decided to go and see for ourselves, without telling our parents, because we were pretty sure they would not allow us to go.

In order to get to the theater, we had to ride our bikes; not too much of a problem for my friend as she lived in the city. It would be a shorter ride for her. However, I lived in the country in a small town called Reeuwijk. There were narrow roads and meadows all surrounded by 11 lakes and small canals. A very quiet, almost deserted area. To ride my bicycle to the city took a good half hour.

So, my friend and I planned to go on a certain afternoon and we were excited to see this frightening new event. The movie started and soon we were both horrified; so scared that we moved to sit on the floor, in between the seats!

We felt more at ease this way and could hide from time to time. And if we felt like watching, we could peek between the seats in front of us. Also, the music gave us the creeps, and from time to time we covered our ears. Needless to say, we were happy when the movie was over.

But now we had to go home. It was almost dark outside, and I had to go the distance on my bicycle, by myself again. My friend did not have that problem remember she lived in the city not far from the theater.

We parted ways and then I realized that I was alone! In my imagination I saw Dracula, looking at me from behind the trees and from the meadows. I must have peddled my bicycle 100 miles an hour to get home. When I reached the corner of the street I lived on, I lost control of my bicycle and drove straight into the canal! I managed to pull out my bike, and soaking wet I reached home—crying, shaking and shivering.

My parents felt sorry for me, but were also angry at me, for disobeying them and going to this horrible scary movie to begin with.

It probably took me a week to lose my fear of possibly seeing Dracula. I checked under my bed and in my closet every night before going to bed. Eventually, I realized that Dracula was not real, and that I did not have to fear him.

Marijke Given

Dracula Fun Facts

1. Bram Stoker never actually visited Transylvania.
2. Bram Stoker's original title for the novel was The Undead.
3. Count Dracula himself is of Hungarian descent and apparently led his troops against the Turks in the 15th Century.
4. Dracula doesn't have a first name and is known simply as Dracula. Dracula means 'devil' in the Wallachian language, in Romanian it's similar to Dracul which means 'Dragon.'
5. Count Dracula's original name was Count Wampyr.
6. There have been over 200 Dracula film roles, 11 of which all starred Christopher Lee in the role of the Count.
7. Throughout the book Dracula's supernatural powers include: hypnosis, telepathic powers, shape-shifting, the ability to create 'mists' and the power to control animals like bats and wolves.

The Moroccan

The fates have thrown me a pickle this time. My business partner, Malik, lay dead in a back alley from a headshot. Through dying blue lips, he tries to tell me who had done it.

We had a lucrative business smuggling arms into Morocco and selling them on the black market. Now more than ever I needed to get out of Tangiers and back to the States; the Moroccan and Spanish police are looking everywhere for me.

I sit at a poker table in a sleazy, back alley bar in a dangerous section of Tangiers trying to win enough money to buy an airplane ticket back home. Sitting across from me is a sinister, filthy little man who smells of bad booze and worse hygiene.

I have known him only as the Moroccan. The red fez atop his head speaks volumes—the Brotherhood. He and they are descendants of the original Berbers and Moors who swept across North Africa centuries ago and into Spain until being turned back by Charlemagne during the reconquest. As I look at the few coins I have left, desperation grips me.

"What's next?" I ask the dealer who sits to my right.

"Seven card stud," he mumbles in a language I have trouble dealing with.

He deals two cards down all around the table, then one up. The dealer throws in one coin.

"Your bet," growls the Moroccan as he stares at me. He hated everything I stood for: America and western civilization.

As I look at my hole cards, my spirits soar. The cards seem to be falling my way.

"I'll see you and raise one," I said as I toss in the last of my money. The unsmiling Moroccan stares at me and said, "I see you and raise you two."

"You know I can't cover that."

"I will take a finger," he says.

In desperation I reply, "Ok."

I turned up my cards, showing a full house. With no immediate response I gleefully reached for the pot.

"Not so fast American," he snarls. He lays down his cards revealing a royal flush.

Smiling, he draws a wicked looking serrated knife from his belt.

"Now I will cut you, American." he says.

I leap to my feet screaming, "If you think I'm going to let you cut me you are crazy!"

Then the two others grab me. One slams my head onto the table with a bloody thwack. The other slams my hand, palm down, onto the table with a thud.

Cheese, these guys are strong.

Then the door burst open and a woman storms into the room with a revolver pointed at the Moroccan's head. "Let the American go," she demands.

This was Tamika, the wife of my dead partner.

A moment of silence follows while the Moroccan calculates his odds.

"Let him go," she repeats as the hammer clicks.

"Let him go," the Moroccan says reluctantly. Finally, they release their grip.

"Besides, I own this place. I won this place from him months ago," she smirks. "Quickly, American. My limo and drivers are waiting outside. They will get you out of the country."

I leap from their grasp and scoop up the pot. As I start for the door, I notice that her right hand is missing its little finger.

Tom Mailey

POKER
HAND RANKINGS

#1 ROYAL FLUSH

#6 STRAIGHT

#2 STRAIGHT FLUSH

#7 THREE OF A KIND

#3 FOUR OF A KIND

#8 TWO PAIR

#4 FULL HOUSE

#9 ONE PAIR

#5 FLUSH

#10 HIGH CARD

BLIND TRUST

editor's note: This is an excerpt from the book-in-progress titled Blind Trust. It is the second story in the book. The first short story can be found in the anthology Senior Moments under the title Happy Endings.

The sun was just going down as I looked out of the small airplane window. The plane was only half full. The sun had colored the skies all around Birmingham, Alabama a bright red iron color. It was the fall of 1970. I had been back in Alabama for a fourteen-day leave, and I was now returning to my ship, the U.S.S. Austin to finish the last six months of my enlistment tour.

For the most part the places I had seen overseas were very friendly places. I had been to cities in France, Spain, and Italy. I could not wait to return to Italy, as I loved Rome more than any other city I had visited by far.

The last six months had been great for me. I had gotten used to working for Chaplain Winters, but for months after taking the job, the Chaplain really pushed hard that I agree to work for him after I got out of the Navy in the Spring of 1971. Chaplain Winters wanted me to go West to Oklahoma and help him achieve his dream ranch. He wasn't due to leave the Navy for a happy retirement for six more years, in 1976. The Chaplain had it all planned out, except he was missing one important thing; his own man that he knew and could be trusted to be the manager, or boss, overseeing his ranch in the meantime. Upon retiring, he planned to return to Oklahoma and take over the ranch. Nothing was ever said about what would happen to his ranch boss.

This all started the day I began my job as a Chaplain's Yeoman, or clerk. He wanted me to be that man. I said from the start that I was against making Oklahoma my new home for six years until he got out of the Navy. After doing the hardest work of setting up and running the ranch, I would have been left high and dry. Homeless, and still not having attended college or getting married, the ranch would have been my new Bride and Wife. In the end, I could not see a future in it for myself, not even a plot of land to farm, or a ranch of my own.

About twice a week for the next six months he would hit me up again to go to Oklahoma and work for him there. Finally, about a month or so before we returned back from a short stop in Norfolk, Virginia, he began his new plan. He was going to replace me as clerk with someone else, who in his eyes, was better than me. I was always telling him he needed to, but not until my time with the Navy was up. But the Chaplain was already making plans to replace me as soon as both of us got back from our leave time at home. But that didn't stop him from hounding me to go start his dream ranch.

When we returned from Norfolk, he flatly asked, no warned me, repeatedly not to go through any of his incoming mail during his six week leave, where back at home he was running from bank to bank trying to get the best interest rates for his dream ranch. Not knowing that when I returned from my own fourteen-day leave that he would have a new Chaplain's clerk, and hopefully future ranch boss, and that I was out of a job.

Chaplain Winters was the man that I knew he was from the start. Even after ordering me time after time to not open any of his mail until his return, despite my protests that the mail would be overflowing and the important stuff needed to be taken care of on time, he was like a bull with his head down and his mind made up. He made sure he would have fourteen days to have me out of my job and the new clerk sitting in my chair when I returned.

It was kind of late, but still before Taps at 9 pm, when I walked on board the Austin. The first thing I did was go to my sleeping area. However, most everyone was still on the mess deck or dining hall watching some kind of spy movie. My two best friends, Marty and Carter, were still up and happy to see me. Marty said that he hated to be the one to tell me, but that I had been replaced as Chaplain's Yeoman. Really, I told him, now that is something I never expected, and asked who the new man was. Carter told me that he had just come aboard the ship a week ago. I asked him if he had time to walk down to his office so we could pull his records and learn more about him. After telling me that it would be against the rules for him to help me because all of his history, awards, and test scores were in his file, Carter asked me to walk with him because he need to make sure he had turned off the office light. When we walked into the office, he told me that the New Guy's file was in the middle top desk drawer, and that he had expected me to want to check out his background. The very first thing I noticed was the state he was from, as I should have expected; the great state of Oklahoma, which was also his nick name. The guy had no experience in office work but grew up on a small ranch. Well, the Chaplain took my advice, but stabbed me in the back as well.

Marty had asked me to let him go through the Chaplain's mail two weeks before the Chaplain got back from leave, and before I left for mine. I flatly told him no, because I had been asked not to, many times. Later, Marty had overheard the Captain asking the Chaplain why he was replacing me, and with his own ears heard Chaplain Winters tell the Captain that for a whole month I did not open one letter for him while he was gone from the ship! The Captain replied that there wasn't anything that could be said except that he did what he had to do. Marty remembered that he had tried to help me with the mail but I had promised not to break my word. What was done was done. The Chaplain may have screwed me, but he could not stop the clock from ticking.

The next morning, I went outside and ran around the flight deck for forty-five minutes. Then I had to move to my new sleeping area, which was full of cook, bakers, and others like myself, who were hired help. We were the sailors that worked with the cooks. I began to learn that I like the way the hours passed by. If I had to do it all over again, I would not mind if I were a full time cook. The cooks worked three meals every other day and were off the other day.

When we came to Malta, I went on a two-day retreat for Christians. Everything was going well until one of the twenty other sailors asked where I was from. I told him near Birmingham, Alabama. Remember, this was 1971 and Birmingham was well known for its race problems. Suddenly the Christian tone changed to bitter words from my Northern Christian friends. I was treated as if I was a K.K.K. member. I got really mad and let out some clean, but unkind words, and the warm Christian retreat turned colder. I refused to be wrongly pigeon holed but did not talk to others unkindly again.

It would burn me up when young women from Spain, France, Italy, and Greece would find out I was from Birmingham and would back up as if I was a bad person. In time I would say I was from somewhere else. I told one very kind and sweet lady once that I was from Red Bay, New York. It did not fool her one bit though because she asked, aren't you from the South? I would change the subject by asking them something about themselves to more things along quicker.

Every night before bed time at Taps, they would show a great movie, and sometimes warn the sailors about bad things that were going down at our next port stop. Now I really paid attention this night. They warned us about two blackmailers, a man and a woman. They were mixing in with the troops and sailors, and when the service man was drunk, they would put him into compromising photographs and then later use them to blackmail them for large sums of money. Sometimes, they would just rob the service men. So far, no deaths had been reported, however the Navy did show us lots of pictures of half-naked service men with a woman who could lure just about anyone she wanted. There was one photo with both the man and the woman together. They were not smiling. As they were showing us the semi-nude photos, I told myself that would never happen to me.

I never get drunk. In Italy, where the café's and bars were all in the same building, one on each side of each other, I stick to the café's. At the end of the presentation, they told us that they believed the man and woman were armed and dangerous and wanted us to be aware.

With all this on my mind, I had decided to ask payroll for seven days of basket leave. I had never been to Venice, Italy, and I was due out of the Navy in three weeks' time. I spoke with the person in charge of payroll, who seemed surprised at my request. Looking the man in the eyes, I told him that for the entire rest of my life I would never get another chance to visit Venice, Italy. Rubbing his head, he smiled and said that is a great reason for wanting basket leave. Continuing, he told me that I would not believe the stories he heard on this job, some of the most unbelievable things. Because you have been truthful with me about your needs, I will grant you your leave, he said, even though I turn down just about everyone. He then told to pick up my seven days' pay whenever I was ready.

I was now glad that I did not get out six months earlier to take a job as a law enforcement officer in Washington, D.C., where it was said no Navy man was turned away for a job. Had I taken the offer, I would have had to sign up for 30 months. I had an entire year's leave time saved up that I could get cashed out in a few weeks when I did get out of the Navy. In that time, I expected to be graduating junior college, at Jefferson State, in Birmingham, Alabama, but until then I knew there might be good looking women to meet and get to know better before my time was up.

I could have made a big mistake a few months earlier. I learned that an American girl that I had been spending time with was only sixteen years old, even though she looked to be in her early twenties. That might have been wishful thinking on my part. Me and about sixty sailors and troops were on a U.S.O. tour bus, and to make the pot sweeter, so were two young American girls. Most of the other men had doing a little skiing for the first time on their minds once we reached our destination, but I had my trained eye on one of the two sisters.

The girls were only interested in finding guys to lay around with in the main building, sitting warmly in someone's loving arms, and watch the record snow fall. There was eight feet of snow on the ground, and it was still falling. Now, one of the other sailors from another ship believed all he would have to do was walk over and take the really cute and well build girl away from me. But I let him know that if he knew what was good for him he would go out and play nicely with the rest of the boys, without a girl to hug and enjoy for the rest of the day. He got angry, but I told my new lady friend that he was mad but would get over it. She liked me coming to her rescue and we quickly returned to kissing each other to death. Everyone else got the message and left us alone the rest of the evening. I could tell that if I was ever alone with her, she planned on doing more than kissing, bless her heart!

I was getting weaker and weaker, and when she told me she had never slept with anyone before, I became even less strong. We were sitting in the back row of the bus on the way to the U.S.S. Austin. Her sister overheard us and threw out a strong statement meant for my ears. She reminded her sister not to forget that she would tell their father everything that went on today, and that to remember that she was only sixteen years old! Her father was the big brass in charge of all the Air Force planes that fly over all of us. I told her, Lora, I am sorry, but because you are so young, all we can do is exchange addresses and we could write each other, even though I did not think I would have done more than I already had with her. But she said No! She was worried I would get back and find someone else and stop writing her. I reminded her that she was what the Navy called "Jail Bait", and that her sister was worse than the F.B.I., being that she was an eye witness to what had gone on today.

When our U.S.O. bus got back to our ship, she wanted to see me again at a local U.S.O. in the city. I said well, it might just be something I will think about, but I knew I would never see her again. I never left the ship that night, and because she wanted to see me, Lora became a stalker. For the next few months she would ride the train up and down Italy's port cities, then go in to U.S.O.'s and find sailors with the U.S.S. Austin patch on his shoulder and ask them to deliver notes to me wanting to hook up. Yes, hook up! Over and over, Lora would send these sad sailors back to me, serving as her pack mules. These sailors, who I had never seen before, were judging me for not hooking up with her and having her Air Force father and sister try to send me to jail for twenty years or more. I asked them all if they would risk their freedom for seven minutes with a nice, cute sixteen-year-old girl, who was also Jail Bait. I wished I would have never seen Lora before, but that was not really true.

The last month before going on basket leave in Venice, I decided to stay on the ship and save money. But then a wild hair must have flown up my mule, because for a minute I asked myself if I was one hundred percent sure I could get away with it, wouldn't it be nice if Lora and I could have seven days in Venice together? No! When God wants me to have a close encounter with the right person, he will close all doors except the one he wants me to walk through. So far, I had been lucky, and talked my way out of anything bad. I had not picked up any unclean thing to follow me the rest of life, and I wanted to keep it that way. So far, so good.

The day before my leave began, I noticed just how many of the higher up's, like the Captain and his C.O., looked me up to say how glad they were that I was taking some time off for myself, and how they wished they too could take off and join me in seeing Venice. Now, here I was in clothing and shoes that were a wet mess from cleaning, talking to the Captain and others like they had nothing else better to do. I made plans through the Captain to start my day at 7 am instead of the 1 pm leave time that all the others who would be leaving for the bars and clubs took.

The next morning, my good friends Carter and Marty seemed so excited they could not contain themselves. They stopped me in the head, or bathroom, to tell me that it looked like my replacement as the Chaplain's Yeoman, O.K., was in hot water with the Chaplain. My two friends said that O.K. had not given in to going to start the ranch when he leaves the Navy and was told that if did not stop all of his mistakes that he would find himself on the cold deck floor, hanging over the side of the ship painting, where you never knew when your day would start or end. Deck hands are on duty twenty-four hours a day. We all believed that to be funny. After all, all O.K. would have to do is walk out of his clean and good sleeping area and go to where the deck hands sleep to notice the wet socks, and that would really turn his head away. And as he walked through, his pace would really pick up faster! What goes around….

Smiling at the memory of that day, I turned my thoughts towards Venice, Italy, as I boarded the train taking me to my last great adventure in the Navy.

Harold Lee Vest

CELESTIAL EVENING

This is her favorite place of reflection and solace she contemplates, as Venus lies suspended in a turquoise pool of cool caressing water. The silky darkness of the night only enhances her escape from the often-cruel reality of her world. Water envelops her body like an aqua elixir of protection. Venus stretches out her arms and legs as far as possible to receive the maximum benefit of the lapping liquid as it engulfs her nude body. With a leisurely motion she shifts her tan shapely legs ever so slightly to allow the wet indigo fingers to massage every inch of her being. Long streaming hair frames her face as her pouty lips part with pleasure. Just as Venus feels the desirable release of inner gratification, some new sensation creeps over her. Dream like other-worldly images flash through her mind. A pulsating rust red orb looks deceptively scorching hot as it brushes past her face. Her blushing cheek is lightly kissed by a misty frost as it crosses. Finally giving in to the unsolicited intrusion, Venus opens her eyes to see who or what obscure being dares interrupt this magical moment. Her flashing violet eyes scrutinize a pulsating reddish solar orb. Two bright moons of splendor also fill the black velvet night sky. Two moons are twice as romantic, sighs Venus. Her floating watery bed is replaced by an intensely cold curtain that shrouds her entire body. "What is this?" she whispers to her enraptured self. "Mars," she hears breathing back in an intoxicating inflection. …
"Mars."

Toni G. Robert

Legend of Lily Flagg

Even though not as old as some homes still standing in Madison County, the Watkins-Moore home on Adams Street bids strongly for a unique place among colorful local history. For this was the location of the only reception ever held for a cow.

In the 1850s the home was built by the Watkins family. James L. Watkins passed the land on to his son, Robert H. Watkins. At the time this home was built, Huntsville was renowned for having some of the most beautiful homes throughout the South. This started a building feud in Huntsville, and Watkins was not to be outdone. He was surrounded by stately dwellings and wanted his home to outshine them all.

As the building of his home began, craftsmen were called in from other states to create plaster of Paris molding. All the woodwork inside the dwelling was made of walnut, and frescoing was put together painstakingly in sections. Slaves were put to work making hand-pressed brick for its walls. Two stairways led to the second floor of the home, with a third going directly to the tower on the roof which consisted of two floors.

There was no other structure like the tower anywhere near Huntsville.

Those who traveled the world spoke of a similar one in Paris. On clear days, one could see as far as the Tennessee River from the lookout in the tower. Robert Watkins built this magnificent home as a gift to his beloved bride, Margaret Carter. She didn't live long in the home, however. Soon after the home was completed, the Civil War began, and the men went away to war. Margaret had just given birth to their first child when Yankee forces reached Huntsville. When the Yankees spread their tents all over the yard of the mansion, the alarmed servants ran in to tell the weakened mother the news. She was extremely agitated and died a few hours after being notified.

When Samuel Moore acquired the home in 1890 he continued to improve the interior of the home. Such rare items as bathtubs, lighting fixtures, and marble mantles from Italy were brought in.

Mr. Moore was quite a colorful character. As a renowned bachelor and member of the state legislature, he loved parties and people. Prominent visitors never missed a tour of his home, and many local celebrities were married there surrounded by flowers and gaiety.

Samuel Moore not only loved people, he loved his cow, Lily Flagg. This was not an ordinary cow but had just returned from the state fair in Chicago where she had taken top honors as the world's greatest butterfat producer. He was as proud of her as if a daughter had taken top honors in a world beauty contest. So, to celebrate her success, he decided to honor her with a grand reception.

He spared no expense in the preparations. He had the home painted a bright yellow for the occasion. A fifty-foot dancing platform was erected at the back of the mansion and was lit by one of the first electric lighting systems in the southeast. Lanterns were hung everywhere, flowers were in abundance.

On the evening of the event, guests dressed in formal attire formed a long line that wound its way to the small stable at the rear of the property where the little Jersey stood, almost hidden by roses. She was honored by people from as far away as Washington.

When the Italian orchestra from Nashville began to play, the dance platform quickly filled up. Special tables were set up all over the property to hold exquisite foods and pastries. Champagne flowed freely, and it is said that this was one of the best parties held in the Huntsville area, before or after. The party lasted until the early morning hours, and older residents said that they would never forget the party for the little cow.

Tom Carney

What did the
mother cow
say to the
baby cow?

"It's *pasture* bedtime."

MARS

Many imagined and were sure that they knew.
But, can you handle what is actually true?
The Bermuda Triangle captures mysteries sunken deep.
Missing ships, planes and cargo she'll keep.
Board with me, if you dare.
Do you want to come back? Or do you care?
Outside of Miami, but not yet San Juan,
Our ship is reeling just before dawn.
Waves are high and wind bursts severe.
What's happened to the atmosphere?
"All below deck!" the captain yelled out.
From the sound of his voice, we had lost our route.
We could see the dread and fear in his eyes.
Shaking his head, as he looked to the skies.
The crew was in danger, this could be it.
To the salty pressure, we had to submit.
Churning and twirling our ship bursts apart.
Crossing my arms, close to my heart.
Suddenly slammed to the ocean floor.
Opening my eyes, I imagined a war.
A microburst unidentified force,
Spewed gas and us on an unexpected course.
"What in the world is that red glow ahead?"
We're going too fast, "It's the landing I dread."
The angry Atlantic spit us up here.
Forcefully soaring, to this new frontier.
The captain called roll, and we're in one piece.
"Please Captain John, just don't sign a lease!"
The Marsdrones smiled and winked their one eye.
We looked puzzled and thought, "Oh My!"
Wide-eyed we glared and weren't quite sure.
Until we knew, their motives were pure.
This planet Mars was a sight to behold.
Not what we thought, with craters and mold.
Mountains of chocolate, flowed into the lake.

The Marsdrones said, "It's yours for the take."
The *Three Musketeers*, not believing this day.
They *Snickered* and looked toward The *Milky Way*.
What are those bumpy bright pills to my side?
Our chewy sweet *Skittles*, just another way that they lied.
Look on that limb of the tall *Twix* tree.
The *M & M* blooms for you and me.
Here on Mars we make, chocolate galore.
White, milk and dark, for all to adore.
The secrets of the *Mars* family chocolate bar.
Caused us, the Marsdrones; to run away far.
People on Earth believe what they are told.
And we support ourselves, from the chocolate they're sold.
The dust they see, don't you know is our cover?
We cause it to pause, to lay there and hover.
The captain you have is a very smart mon'.
We heard he was wise like Solomon.

Sorry for your tumbling triangular trip.
We had to do it to capture your ship.
It's turbulent out there in the Atlantic so deep.
Our Military has ships and planes that we keep.
Don't believe everything that you hear.
The Marsdrones are watching, and you could disappear!

**Inspired by John Carson and The Milky Way Farm
1930 Mars Family built the farm (2,800 acres) in Pulaski, Tennessee
Mars Corporation: Milky Way, Snickers, Skittles, Three Musketeers, Mars Bars,
M & M's, Twix

Belinda Talley

Gutenberg Woes

The captain has beamed back to earth for an emergency. Belan the doctor is sick and Chris the first officer is having a nervous breakdown. What next? After those thoughts run through my mind, there is a squeal, sparks start dancing on the console on the command deck. Then all goes silent and black. All systems have shut down. The ship has stopped dead in space. We don't move, for we can't see. It's total blackness. Then the emergency lights come on.

My communicator by my side is dead. The elevators are not working so we are stuck. I know there will be people in a panic on the ship. How can I communicate to them? Oh! Why did we leave earth before this ship was completely built? Can't change that now. Have to go from here.

All of us on the bridge realize that Captain Carson can't beam back. We must fix all the problems ourselves. How can we contact engineering?

The captain had mentioned something about a panel on the wall if something goes wrong. I go and find the panel and inside. There is a list on the door. There are emergency procedures for all kinds of things. In case of fire see page ten. Flood, page twenty. In case of infestation, page thirty. In case of alien contact, war in space, ah! Here it is "loss of power."

In this section it is broken down even more. To gain communication within the ship, to get elevators useable, food, water and waste availability, heating and cooling, lighting systems, transport system, maneuverability, and communication with earth.

Many are in despair and have no hope. I want to get back their hope. I also see inside the panel a hand-held communicator directly to engineering. It is run separately form the ships, so it works. My voice comes on into engineering. The main engineer's voice comes back over my communicator and finds out how we are talking. I put him on the job to get the elevators working first. I go down the list, just as it is in the book. It is listed by importance.

There are panels all over the ship with these communicators. Soon all the working people that can fix parts of the ship have one. I say to all. "I encourage everyone to work together. If you see a problem or something isn't right, don't try and fix it yourself, get someone to help. It will get fixed faster that way."

We get the elevators to work by hand, until the mechanics can fix the electrical problem. The engineers get working on the heating and cooling system. Some mechanics and plumbers are on the food, water, and waste. Lighting is being overseen by electricians. Scientists are needed for transport. To get the ship moving again we get engineers and computer experts. Last but not least, communications with Earth. It needs electricians and computer experts. After all, the ship is run mostly by computer.

It took over a week and lots of arguments, but all was finally working again.

Over Earth's communications come out captain 's voice. "Hey! Where is everyone? I've been calling and calling." We tell him that we must have just missed his calls. He asks if everything is okay and tells us he is ready to beam back on board. We said everything is fine. And we then proceeded to beam him back on board.

When he materializes on the transporter, we just stare. We know he is our captain from his eyes, the color of his hair and the hat on his head, but the clothes were just hanging on his thin skeletal frame. Our captain, when he left, was at least two hundred and fifty pounds. Somehow the transporter had not beamed aboard his water-soluble fat.

The captain sees us staring and says, "What are you looking at?" Then he looks down at himself and gasps. With surprise he says, "What a way to go!" then he looks up and asks, "Did something happen to the transporter while I was gone?"

Margaret J. Forrest

SPACE TRIVIA TWO

15. What name was given to the invisible material once thought to occupy all space?

16. Which is the largest moon in the solar system?

17. Where, theoretically, might one find objects squeezed to an infinite density?

18. Which is the largest moon of Saturn?

19. Who discovered Uranus?

20. Which is the largest planet in the solar system?

21. What is the smallest planet in the solar system?

22. Which is the brightest comet in the solar system?

23. What would you find if you travelled to the center of the solar system?

24. Which planet is named after the Roman goddess of love?

25. What kind of extraterrestrial object has been named after the 17th-century astronomer Edmond Halley?

26. What was the first artificial satellite?

27. What is the name of the space shuttle destroyed in midair 28 Jan 1986?

28. Where is the chromosphere?

29. What, ultimately, will the sun become?

(answers page 153)

GREAT-GRANDDAD'S TALE

With Christmas dinner over
In the house at the edge of the wood
We were all stuffed like Santa Claus
And feeling mighty good.

Great-Granddad rose from his chair
And went to the window sill
Said I'll tell you all a story
If you promise to be still.

And all of the little ones
Gathered round his chair
As Great-Granddad lit his pipe
And took on an important air.

The grownups took their places
All around the room
As Grandmama hung up her towel
And put away her broom.

She doused the lights one by one
And lit the Christmas tree
Then took the rocker next to his
And put a child upon her knee.

When all was still and silent
The old man began his yarn
About the night in Nineteen-Nine
Out behind the barn.

Twas a cold, cold night in December
A clear and snowless night
I had just put away old Bessie
And locked the barn up tight.
When my brother came a runnin'

And shoutin' out my name
He bolted down the path
And over the fence he came.

'What in tarnation…?'
I said as he went by
But he just kept on runnin'
And pointin' to the sky.
And then I looked up and saw it
And I froze right to the spot
There was a ball of fire comin'
And looking mighty hot!

He had heard all about it
Down at the General Store
They say it comes every seventy-six
And never less or more.

'It's Halley's Comet up there
A hangin' in the sky
They say it's comin' mighty close
You can touch it if you try.'

Well, the fireball was closin' in
With a tail a mile long
I climbed the barn up to the roof
Though I knew that it was wrong.

His head was mighty hot
And his tail a path of ice
And I jumped aboard that comet
That few would ever see twice.

Yes, sir, I mounted that tail
A hangin' on for my dear life

And I dug in with a pick—
My good ol' huntin' knife.

That comet was a raging bull
But I rode him just the same
We left the Earth far behind
And to the Moon we came.

I wanted to stop and use my knife
To cut a hunk of cheese
But that comet wasn't hungry
And we flew by like the breeze.

We flew by Mars and Jupiter
And then past Saturn too
That comet kept right on goin'
Trying to shake you-know-who!

And then I started thinkin'
I'd better be headin' back
Before that loco comet
Jumped right off its track!

I jumped off on an asteroid
That was driftin' lazy by
And then I caught another one

That was hangin' in the sky.

One by one I made my way
Back to good ol' Earth
And rode down on a meteor
And jumped for all my worth.

I aimed myself best as I could
Hoping my landing would be soft
And crashed down through the roof
Into my very own hay loft!

The children started laughing
When the old man finished his yarn
About the night in Nineteen-Nine
Out behind the barn.

Great-Granddad just stood and smiled
And pointed to the sky
And out the window we could see
Old Halley's going by.

Then out the door he hurried
Though we told him come inside
"I can't!" he said as he jumped up
And took old Halley's for a ride!

John Evan Carson

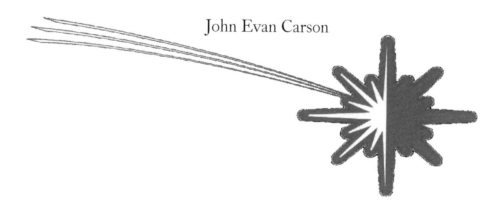

Tribute to Genie

My engineering career began in Alaska and ended in Huntsville, Alabama. It encompassed many exceedingly interesting jobs and facilitated world-wide travels in both directions. Its demise was not due to the lack of further interesting job opportunities, but to my personal dilemma at the time. I would not have said so then, but in retrospect I had reached that cliché-termed "mid-life crisis."

I was in the process of getting a divorce when I met Genie, who was also divorced. This is that wonderful woman who would change my life completely. But our relationship had not yet fully developed when the time came for me to move to a new job. I resigned from my job and worked on the relationship. We were married on Thanksgiving Day in 1973 and spent almost 43 years together before Alzheimer's took her away on September 21, 2016.

***

My perplexity with our relationship is reflected in the poem "What Do You Want from Me", written in early October 1973. The question was resolved the next month as we wrote our own vows for the wedding. The minister, Harry Pritchett, played his ukulele and sang "Morning Has Broken" for us. (I must confess breaking into tears as I pause my writing to check out the song which I remember as "Blackbird has Spoken" on YouTube.)

"The Rainbow of Love", written 25 years later, still stands today as the keynote for 43 wonderful years with Genie.

The hospice nurse said that we had to stop feeding Genie because she had difficulty swallowing. Feeding her could lead to aspiration and pneumonia. I had to accept that we could not save her, and I had to give her permission to go. This I did reading "Genie's Leaving Me" to her.

"Let the Tears Flow" represents just a bit of my grieving. I no longer shed a tear every day, but from time to time a few tears will ease down my cheeks. I don't fight it. If there is a gusher like when I was putting this down on paper, I sit back from the keyboard and let it flow.

***

Since Genie left me, the cleaning lady has been going through the clutter accumulated over the years. Some of the treasures from our travels find a new display spot. Obvious junk ends up in the weekly trash. If there is a question, the material is brought to me for that hard decision: Keep or trash? Recently, a large plastic bin full of papers was referred to me. The contents bore dates between 2002 and 2010; post-retirement and pre-Alzheimer's. There were many catalogs, old doctor bills, copies of orders, lists of who got what for Christmas; mostly disposable trivia but also a bit of memorabilia. It was the latter that caught my attention.

I found a faded typewritten list of aphorisms. "Miss Genie Turner, Monday" at the top of the sheet dates the paper in Genie's late teens or early twenties, the age at which we begin knowingly or unknowingly to shape our philosophy of life.

What we read has subtle influences which are strengthened if we take the time to copy and reread them. Placing then in a protective cover a half-century later is further affirmation of their effect. I noted with a smile three items with a little checkmark beside them, no doubt added at a latter review.

Further evidence of their purpose and effect was the inclusion of the poem, "What We Live By" by Louis Redmond, within that same protective cover. It is not included here because of its length, but I have selected a few excerpts to illustrate my point.

Among Genie's papers I frequently found copious notes on some book that she had been reading or on a documentary which she may have watched on PBS. Then one day I came across five pages of her handwriting on a yellow pad. Flawless fluid writing, single spaced, with no breaks. I had never seen her copy any material and this appeared to be something that flowed directly from her mind to paper in a smooth flow of descriptive words. I could not avoid the vernacular: It blew my mind.

It was difficult for me to understand how Genie could have conceived of this story situated in East Africa during World War I. However, her undergraduate major had been history before she went into audiology and teaching the hearing-impaired for her graduate degree. I had also observed her strong interest in World War II history. So, I was ready to attribute to her this insightful story of the impact on a native accustomed to battling with spears, being forced to lay down his familiar weapon and take the gun pushed into his hands by the colonial powers.

Fortuitously, my step-daughter Gina stopped by one evening. As I was telling her about finding this fantastic story in her mother's handwriting, Gina asked what it was about. I started to describe the story. "Oh, yes," she said, "I remember that well." I had a fleeting moment of gratification at hearing this confirmation. Then came the rest of the story.

Genie loved *West with the Night* and often talked to Gina about it. She also bought a paper-back version as a gift for Gina, not wanting to give up her hard-cover copy. Gina loved the book, so much so that she went on Amazon and bought an eBook version of it. She had the eBook with her the evening she visited. Flipping her finger across the screen, she found the story I was referring to. Word for word it was in chapter 8 of Beryl Markham's book.

No longer able to attribute this wonderful story to a flow from Genie's mind, I still refer to it in this "Tribute to Genie". The history, the culture, the moral about warfare were all clearly embedded in that mind as it copied five hand-written pages word for word.

***

I loved to travel. I loved to travel for the simple ambience of foreign venues. In my personal travels I avoided the luxury hotels that provided American conveniences and food any place in the world; for a price. I walked the back streets and alleys finding where the natives ate, eating what the natives ate, drinking what the natives drank, learning a few phrases in the native tongue to interact with them on the most basic level. I slept in fields, on hillsides, on beaches, or sought a room for a few dollars, or upgraded to the occasional budget hotel.

Genie also loved to travel, but she pleaded with me not to choose any place rated less than two stars in Eastern Europe. She wanted a bath in the room, not down the hall.

Not to worry, on our travels we would occasionally chance upon a wonderful little Gasthaus tucked away in the woods. And the companies I worked for selling insurance in the military marketplace always rewarded their most productive agents with an annual trip for a "business meeting" in an interesting or sometimes even exotic location with five-star accommodations.

Genie wrote extensive letters to her parents (fortunately preserved) describing those trips to Rothenburg an der Taube, Mallorca, Malta, Lisbon, Amsterdam, Paris, Garmisch, Vienna, Salzburg, San Francisco, Lake Tahoe, Hong Kong, and others. We also visited friends in London and Rome and took a tour of Florence and the wine countryside of Tuscany.

After the wall came down in 1989, we traveled extensively in Eastern Europe to Budapest, Bratislava, Prague, Pilsen, and small towns in-between. We usually drove our Citroen, which would sit down with a sigh at the end of the day as its hydraulic suspension system settled down to rest for the night. I was careful, of course, to seek out three-star hotels so that we had the requisite facilities in our room.

Wherever we went, Genie was sure to search out the souvenir shops. I recall our first trip into Czechoslovakia in the fall of 1989. Genie was at a meeting in Erlangen (near Nurnberg) for the directors of the child-care centers in Germany. When the meeting ended on a Friday afternoon, Alice Rose, a colleague, joined us in a trip to Karlovy Vary (the once world-famous spa of Karlsbad). Their first quick check revealed that the shops had different opening hours. While I went up to the room to rest, the two of them went with paper and pen in hand to note exactly what time each shop opened. They were up early Saturday morning to hit all the stores in sequence as fast as they could. They soon learned that they had similar tastes and there was a rush to see who could find the goodies first as supplies were limited. Alice became a very good friend. She and her husband joined us on a tour to Moscow and Leningrad the next year where the ladies scoured the shops for lacquerware.

As a result of diligent shopping techniques, we have an eclectic collection of "stuff". I don't even know the names of half of them. There are many prints from Germany, more prints and posters from all over; the Louvre in Paris, colorful Chodsko vases and crystal ware from Czechoslovakia, straw figures, mud figures, exquisite Lladro figurines from Spain, Christmas dinnerware from Waechtersbach, pottery from Alsace, lacquerware from Russia, and the list goes on, if only I knew what to call them all.

Once again, tears roll involuntarily down my cheeks. I have come to realize, in writing this tribute to Genie, that all those catalogs that filled our mailbox week after week were her travel brochures as she settled down to the mundane work-a-day world. And they were her "souvenir shops," which she scoured for the little more beauty from the creative hands in far off lands.

***

Amongst the clutter that I have gone through, I found a book that Gina had given her mother on how to *de-clutter*. I am a "clutterer" myself, so I didn't read the book in its entirety. However, in scanning the volume, I found an interesting section of highlighted material. The author had labeled the problem of cluttering to be a "hoarding" complex. Typically, one page listed the cons, one page listed the pros. The solution was to do an evaluation of the pros and cons.

The con side had six or seven items highlighted. On the pro side there was only one single line highlighted: "It gives me pleasure."

I need no list of pros or cons to evaluate our life together. Genie gave me pleasure. I am also taking pleasure in looking at all the treasures that gave *her* pleasure. What is a little clutter when it serves as a reminder of 43 wonderful years?

Bill Holman

WHAT DO YOU WANT OF ME?

What do you want of me?

Two steamboats passing in the night,
Toot their horns, pass to the right,
Comforted to know that they are not alone
In the fog.

But what do You want of me?

Shall I pass to the right?
Toot my horn?
Cast anchor? Weigh anchor?
Be gone in the night?

What do you want of me?

Be gone in the night?
Be gone in the night!
Let your presence be gone
Before dawn's early light.
Be gone! Be gone in the night.

Is That what you want of me?

Bill Holman
October 1973

THE RAINBOW OF LOVE

Roses are red, violets are blue.
They make a pretty array,
But with colors too few
To properly portray
The spectrum of my love for you.

It takes the rainbow of love,
Every color, every hue
With clouds white as a dove
In the azure blue sky above
To display how much I love you.

Meld yellow and brown for a golden
crown
To adorn the head I adore. Ah,
Then add sparking sequins to your
gown
So when you dance, a swirling aurora
Borealis brightens my life.

Yellow jonquils and daffodils;
Green valleys midst purple hills
Where the yellow warbler trills.
I love you, my darling, still
I love you and always will.

Passionate purple, a beautiful hue,
Shades of lavender, violet and blue.
Darling, my darling, how I love you.
As the aroma of orange blossoms fill
The air, I take you my wife for life.

Roses are red, violets are blue.
But what is the color, what is the hue?
Where is the rainbow of my love for
you?

There it is for the world to see.
It's all the colors of you and me.

Bill Holman

GENIE'S LEAVING ME

Genie's leaving me

I am grieving her leaving

It's OK for you to die

It's OK for me to cry

We two must say good-bye

Genie is going away

I am going to stay

I must give you permission to go

And give myself permission to go on

I pray you stay a little longer

I love you so

I don't want you to go.

But it's OK.

Bill Holman

9/19/2016

Let the tears flow

Every day I shed a tear

It keeps my vision clear

Though there's sadness in my heart

That we had to part

The flow of tears

Pays tribute to the years

We had together

So I let the tears flow

And I let them show

To let you know

I loved you so.

Bill Holman

11/4/16

THE THINGS WE LIVE BY

By Louis Redmon

Excerpts from a poem saved amongst Genie Holman's memorabilia:

Contrasts make a life…

Contrasts, walking arm in arm, make a man.

He stares at the sea's edge and the tempting joint

    of earth and sky, drawn to the places where

    he can put himself beyond all help,

    but his own.

Love flows like a river through the center of life.

Tenderness and love make life.

A man can't live bottled up.

What he is must be let out into the world.

We live most of all by giving life.

We plant a flower, have a baby, paint a picture, make

    a chair and put something into life that was not

    there before

And we leave our signature on the world.

Biographies

And we leave our signature on the world.

Belinda Talley loves to hear people laugh and feels that she was created with a passion for joy. As a Laughter Therapist she looks for the humor in any situation. Seventeen years of experience in the retirement industry provided her with some slippery situations and clever characters for her first book, to be released in 2019. She moved from Gadsden as a child, when her parents, Tom and Buna German started a fabric business in Huntsville. The Cloth Basket stitched memories together in the lives of our community for thirty-five years. Belinda and Tom, were married on The Guntersville Bridge in 1970, and now reside in Huntsville, Alabama. Their children Brent & Meredith (Texas) and Adriane & Jason (Florida) have given them five glorious grandchildren. "The Good Lord gave me the dream, my seniors delivered the drama, family and friends applauded my attempts and my sister pushed me to produce. My writing instructors encouraged me and each one had a part in constructing my creativity, for this I am grateful. A wise man once taught me that you can only cook from what is in your cupboard. You draw from your life experiences, what you have walked through, the people in your path, love stolen and love given, tears of tragedy and laughing to tears. Thank you, John Carson for noticing the colorful gift that God planted inside of me." **Selections in book include "Don't Push It" (4), "Opposites Attract" (28), "The Treasure" (93), and "Mars"(130).**

Betty Pettigrew's best subject has always been English and reading her best escape. Born in a small, rural farming community in Colorado, she had only been out of the state to Wyoming until she married a sailor and took off for San Francisco. They were a Navy family and lived in lots of places including Hawaii. Their travels took them to Europe and Japan, so there were lots of experiences unusual to her upbringing. Betty says, "I wrote about all of them in one way or another. Sometimes ideas just float through my head and have to be captured by adding them to a journal or other written form. *Creative writing makes me happy.*" **Selections in the book include "The Party Line" (13) and "Balloons Float Up" (82).**

Bill Homan has a BA (Math and German) and a BS (EE) from the University of Alaska, and an MS (Systems Management) from USC. He has lived and worked in Germany, Japan, Turkey and Alaska (with a summer on the arctic slope in Canada). He loves travel and has made it around the world in both directions. Bill has used at least a dozen different languages in his world-wide travels. In his mid-90's, this eternal student is still taking classes and teaching classes at the senior center in Huntsville, Alabama. **Selection in the book include "A Tribute to Genie" (137).**

Carol Wells Barnette came to appreciate tongue twisters and poetry in high school. With tongue twisters she wanted her readers to participate in exercise of the tongue before speaking, poetry to share with readers as an extended family. She has taken several classes in writing at Columbia College and extended that knowledge through private classes to include one at the Huntsville Senior Center. She was raised between Arizona and California but now makes her home in Lacey's Spring Alabama. **Selections in the book include "The Grist Mill" (27), "Tongue Twister Tales" (48), and "The Midnight Tree" (92).**

Elizabeth Brown is a naturally creative person stays very busy and she loves it! In addition to her writing, she crochets, knits, weaves carpets, makes quilts, and works in the wood shop. When not busy making gifts for her very large family and circle of friends she enjoys playing Scrabble at the senior center. **Selection in the book include "Summer 2018" (74).**

Ernest "Skipper" Colin lived in NM until after collage. He moved to Huntsville, AL in 1963 and retired in 1995 after nearly 33 years with Teledyne Brown Engineering. **Selection in the book include "Chief Sunny Skies" (64).**

Georgia Everson lives in Huntsville, Alabama. She has attended creative writing classes at the senior center on and off for the last ten years. She is active in her church and is involved in many activities at the senior center. **Selection in the book include "On How Things Have Changed" (10).**

Harold Lee Vest was born in Walker County, Alabama in the small town of Quinton in 1949. He served in the Navy from 1969-1971. In 1972 he enrolled at Jefferson State in Birmingham, Alabama. Among other things, he has been a professional photographer, coal miner, and foster dad along with his late wife, Rita Kaye Vest, PhD., and now is pursuing his lifelong dream of becoming an author. **Selections in the book include "Making Pictures Out of Words" (61), "My Own Path to Real True Love..." (87), "The Christmas Purse" (104), and "Blind Trust" (117).**

John E. Carson is a regular contributor to the *Old Huntsville Magazine*, and the author of twelve published novels, with more in the works, and many poems in print and on public display. He is also an integral part of the company he helped found, CBA Publishing Services, LLC. John serves on the Honor Guard for the American Legion Post 237 and is an advocate for Pets for Vets. His ultimate goal is to see a chapter opened in Huntsville, Alabama to serve the Tennessee Valley. He teaches Creative Writing in Huntsville, Alabama where he lives with his wife and co-author, Marlene, and trusty dog, Mr. Freckles. **Selections in the book include "U.F.O.'s" (Credits Page), "Introduction" (1), "Breakfast on Mars" (3), "Ninety-Eight and Counting" (25), "The Honor Box" (79), "Leon the Lazy Angel" (97), "Great-Granddad's Tale" (135), and "Special Thanks" (154).**

Margaret Joan Forrest was born and raised in Wilmington, Massachusetts. She has two wonderful daughters. The oldest is married and has 7 children. The younger one is married and just had her first child. She has traveled extensively in the United States and Canada. Margaret went to college in Utah and lived in Nova Scotia where her children were born. She moved to Alabama from Canada in 1987, mainly to get away from the ice and snow. She has had many jobs, some of which included modeling, acting, singing telegrams, costume courier, weather graphics for channel 31 WAAY TV, and teaching. Growing up, she always loved to write until she got to college and took a writing course in which her first paper was commented on by the teacher, "You will never be a writer." After that she just wrote for herself and kept a daily journal. She says, "Now here I am many years later in another writing class and this time I'm loving it." **Selections in the book include "Venus: The Love Shack" (99) and "Gutenberg Woes" (132).**

Marijke Given lives in Huntsville, Alabama with her bird, Schatze. She was born in Indonesia and grew up in Holland. She met her husband, who was an American, in Spain and moved to the United States shortly after getting married. Marijke has two daughters, Monique and Wendy, and a 26-year-old grandson, Derik. She has lived all over this country, and finally settled in Huntsville almost 30 years ago. She has made it her mission to write her mother's story of being in a Japanese concentration camp during WWII with her new-born daughter. **Selections in the book include "Marijke's Story" (50), and "Dracula" (112).**

M.D. Smith worked from 1958 until 1999 in the Radio and Television business with his parents who had been in the business for much of their lifetimes. He has written many stories about the WAAY Radio and TV days and special events, many of which didn't turn out quite like expected. M.D. has been Amateur Radio operator WA4DXP since 1962 and still enjoys the hobby. He built a lot of his own equipment. He was General Manager of WAAY-TV for 36 years. M.D. and Judy Smith, having raised eight children, seven sons and a daughter, could write many volumes involving just the kids during their 57-year marriage. **Selection in book include "Pilot in Command" (65).**

Patricia Ann Woolfork "Trishann" is a Newark, NJ native, a graduate of Weequahic High and received her BA Magna cum laude from Kean University. As "Trishann", she has written hundreds of poems, essays, and short stories. To date, she has sold over 240 copies of her self-published collection of poetry, and this revised edition has some of her latest works as well as the first poems ever written as a high school teenager. This proud mother of three adult children and nine grandchildren continues to write and perform. Look for her latest book of poetry to come out soon. **Selections in the book include "Road Trip Parts 1&2" (21), "Those Were the Good Old Days" (32), "The Opportunity of a Lifetime" (70), and "Monument, Colorado" (108).**

Rick Dowell lives in Huntsville, Alabama and is a regular member of the Creative Writing Class. He enjoys spending time in nature and is a skilled poet who has been writing for many years. He can often be seen with his notebook and pencil in hand. **Selection in the book include "My Little Radio" (78).**

Sally Rogers has a 73-year history of no formal writing experience. Having been born and raised on the family farm in rural America, attending a one-room school during grades 1-8, she graduated from a consolidated country high school and now has stories to write. She continued her education at vocational and technical schools and community colleges. Her career path took her to work for the State of Wisconsin, Motorola and Walmart. Having vast experience and traveling many roads, she pulled from her country life to write a story about a bullfrog outside her window. This story is dedicated to her family and six grandchildren who without them she would not have been inspired to write. **Selection in the book include "Hey! Mr. Bullfrog You Are Back"(34).**

Sandy (Shafer) Ballas and her husband of 26 years moved to the Huntsville area January of 2017. Sandy didn't know what she wanted to be when she grew up until she took the Creative Writing class at the Huntsville Senior Center. She had worked at so many different jobs until she retired from the Government 10 years ago. Travel Clerk, Computer Aide, Math Aide, Firefighter, Living History and Fire Dispatcher were all Government jobs for the Navy, Air Force, Army and the Park Service. Now she is pursuing writing as her passion. **Selections in the book include "Hope" (9), "A True Untold Story" (16), and "Retniw Nam Dlo" (105).**

Thomas Mailey obtained his Ph. D. from the University of Pittsburgh. He is a retired assistant professor and Operations Research Analyst currently residing in Huntsville, Alabama and attending the creative writing class at the senior center. **Selections in the book include "POTUS vs The Prime Minister" (12), "The Longest 76 Hours" (44), and "The Moroccan" (114).**

Toni Robert is a retired school teacher who now operates her handmade natural stone jewelry business. She resides with her husband and Toy Aussie. Toni recently joined the Creative Writing class. Along with writing, camping, hiking, swimming, and kayaking are also her passions. **Selections in the book include "Different Lives, Different Faces" (68), and "Celestial Evening" (126).**

Tom Carney Dec. 15, 1946 - June 16, 2011
Tom Carney was born in the Hurricane Creek area and was a lifelong resident of Huntsville. Tom was owner and publisher of *Old Huntsville Magazine*, along with his wife Cathey, since 1989. In addition, Tom has two published books, *The Way It Was*, recently re-released and *Portraits in Time*, coming in 2019. He assisted other authors with several more local books. He won numerous awards over the years for his writing and is nationally renowned for his historical contributions. **Selections in the book include "The Battle of Huntsville" (83), and "Legend of Lily Flagg" (127).**

Answers to Space Trivia and Space Trivia Two

1. Gravity.
2. Venus.
3. Mars.
4. Mercury.
5. Mercury and Venus.
6. Venus.
7. Moon.
8. Yuri Gagarin.
9. Pioneer 10.
10. Four: Columbia, Endeavour, Discovery, Atlantis.
11. 5,800 K (5.,530 C).
12. Gravity.
13. The sun.
14. Mercury.

15. Ether.
16. Ganymede.
17. Black Hole.
18. Titan.
19. William Herschel.
20. Jupiter.
21. Pluto.
22. Halley's comet.
23. The Sun.
24. Venus.
25. A Comet.
26. Sputnik 1.
27. Challenger.
28. Sun.
29. A white dwarf.

Answers to word puzzles:

Page 20: Jimmy Hoffa is not dead. He works at the National Enquirer with Elvis and Bigfoot.

Page 33: To boldly go where no one has gone before.

Page 82: These are the voyages of the Starship Gutenberg.

SPECIAL THANKS

This anthology would not have been possible without the help and support of many people; Anna Talyn Carson, President of Product Design and Marketing for CBA Publishing Services, LLC for the incredible cover design and Christine Brown for the Layout and Editing of this anthology chief among them, for their many hours of hard work and service.

*

To our Sponsors:

Harold Lee Vest

and

CBA Publishing Services, LLC

*

To our Guest Speakers:

Skip Vaughn, Editor of *The Redstone Rocket*

And author of *Vietnam Revisited*

and

Cathey Carney, Publisher of the

Old Huntsville Magazine

*

To the Officers of the U.S.S. Gutenberg:

1st Officer—Christine Brown, President and Editor-In-Chief

Ships Doctor—Belinda Talley

*

Special Mention to Don and Dorothy Howard for their past appearance and inspiring talk, and the donation of four prints of famous authors that have watched over every class for the last two years.

This class would not be possible without the support of Becky Rollston, Activities Coordinator for the Huntsville-Madison County Senior Center.

And to all the members of the class and crew of the Star Ship Gutenberg who continue to amaze and inspire me with their creativity and talent.

To all the authors who have contributed to this volume special thanks are due to you as well.

And finally, to you the reader, without who none of this would be possible, a hearty thank you from all of us.

Thank you all; fair winds and Godspeed!

John E. Carson

Made in the USA
Columbia, SC
05 November 2018

FROM THE BEGINNINGS OF THE WRITTEN WORD ON CLAY TABLETS OVER 5,600 YEARS AGO, TO JOHANNES GUTENBERG'S INVENTION OF MOVABLE TYPE AND THE PRINTING PRESS, TO TODAY'S ELECTRONIC TABLETS AND COMPUTERS, MANKIND HAS BEEN ON A JOURNEY OF ENLIGHTENMENT THAT HAS ENCOMPASSED UNTOLD THOUSANDS OF VOYAGES THROUGH LIFE ON EARTH AND PAST THE BOUNDARIES OF OUR SOLAR SYSTEM INTO THE FAR REACHES OF THE MILKY WAY GALAXY.

THE INVENTION OF WRITING HAS GIVEN US THE POWER TO TRANSMIT PICTURES, IDEAS, HISTORY AND LEARNING FROM ONE PERSON TO ANOTHER, ONE GENERATION TO ANOTHER AND INSPIRE AND INFLUENCE CULTURES AND CIVILIZATIONS ACROSS THE GLOBE.

THE ABILITY TO WRITE CREATIVELY, TO DRAW AND HOLD AN AUDIENCE THROUGH STORIES WRITTEN AND READ IS ONE OF THE GREATEST GIFTS GIVEN TO HUMANKIND; AND THE 2018 CREATIVE WRITING CLASS HAS PRESENTED THEIR UNIQUE AND DIVERSE TALENTS IN THIS ANTHOLOGY, TAKING US WITH THEM AS THEY TRANSCEND THE WALLS OF THE CLASSROOM, CROSS BORDERS BOTH REAL AND IMAGINARY AND EVEN MOVE FORWARD OR BACK THROUGH TIME ITSELF.

TRAVEL WITH US NOW AS WE BOLDLY GO WHERE NO CREATIVE WRITING CLASS HAS GONE BEFORE!

VOYAGES: AN ANTHOLOGY
Class of 2018

cbapub.com

CBA
PUBLISHING
SERVICES, LLC

ISBN 9781732474628

9 781732 474628